# The Power of Your Choices

# The Power of Your
# CHOICES

### How Your Choices Can Impact
### Your Destiny and Your Life

## —— Hardy Clayton ——

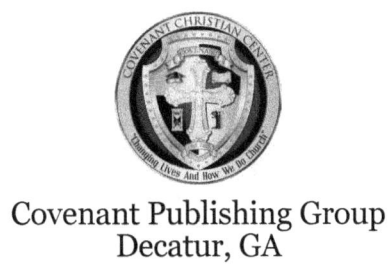

Covenant Publishing Group
Decatur, GA

The Power of Your Choices:
How Your Choices Can Impact Your Destiny and Your Life

Copyright © 2017 Covenant Publishing Group

All rights reserved.

No part of this book may be reproduced or transmitted in any form or by any means, electronic or mechanical, including photocopying, recording or by any information storage and retrieval system, without written permission from the publisher, except for the inclusion of brief quotations in a review

Address inquiries to the publisher:

> Covenant Publishing Group
> 3040 Lauren Parc Road
> Decatur, Georgia 30032

ISBN: 978-0-9990392-0-5 (print)
ISBN: 978-0-9990392-1-2 (ebook)

Library of Congress Control Number: 2017960527

Printed in the United States of America

# Preface

Life as we have come to know it is neither just a simple lap around the track, a 400-meter dash, nor a marathon. It is a journey. And as we go through this journey called life, we are faced with peaks, valleys and numerous life experiences that will have a profound impact on how we view life and live on a daily basis. Every choice in life affects our careers, relationships, and ultimately, our destiny because it's all interconnected.

I was inspired to write this essay, which eventually turned into a book, because I started journaling about my life. Journaling caused me to slow down long enough to do some serious self-reflection. Even though I was not keenly aware of what I was doing, I was actually starting the process of finding my life's purpose while embarking on a journey that would help me live a more balanced, fulfilling life.

Neuroscientists have conducted studies that indicate that some of us operate on automatic pilot; therefore, when this happens, little thought goes into our decisions, which could lead to following a path that could be destructive. Bad decision-making can also determine how we view the world based on previous experiences or our limited exposure to the world as a whole.

This negative pattern of making key decisions is a way of life for most of us, and I was no exception. As I mentioned earlier, this literary experience did not come about as result of wanting to make money, simply having my name in print, or a history making good decisions. In fact, it came about after I experienced decades of making poor decisions despite being recognized as having higher-than-average intelligence.

According to some standardized testing, I was identified as having enough intellectual ability to be placed in some advanced classes when I was in the sixth grade. This was an eye-opening experience for me because previously there was never any indication that my academic skills or abilities were any different than anyone else's skills. In fact, the pack mentality, or the most popular choices, dominated my thinking, and I flowed with my environment. If one of my friends wanted to be a professional athlete, then I wanted to be a professional athlete. If one of my friends thought schoolwork was whack, then I thought schoolwork was whack as well. At this age, I had no idea that my environment impacted most of my decisions. In other words, there was mental shaping taking place that would prepare me for how I would function later in life unless there was a radical disruption in this negative pattern of thinking.

Coming face-to-face with a major disruption in my life caused me to realize that the blueprint I was building my life on needed some adjustments because my pattern of thinking was ineffective. Despite my identified above-average skill sets, the life that I was building was going to crumble right before my very eyes if I didn't change my mindset from a conformist to an individualist.

I am a realist; therefore, I clearly understand that reading this book is not going to fix your life or cause you to miraculously change how you have been living. However, it is my desire that this book challenges you to be more reflective, intentional, contemplative, and critical, which will lead you to make better choices. A friend of mine said it best when he said, "My job is not to save you, but my job is to simply challenge you to think. And if I can get you to think, you will save yourself."

I hope that you find this book interesting, entertaining, and challenging so that you can move beyond any self-imposed limitations and begin the journey to finding your purpose and living a balanced life.

~Hardy Clayton

# Contents

*Preface, v*
*Acknowledgements, xi*
*Introduction, xiii*

1. **The Awakening** ............................................................. 1
   A Clearer Picture ............................................................. 6
2. **Like a Grasshopper** ..................................................... 9
   Running with Horses ...................................................... 19
3. **Road to Redemption** ................................................. 21
   Hostages of Past Kings................................................... 27
4. **Resurrected Dreams** ................................................. 31
   Hiding from Destiny ....................................................... 40
5. **Forest for the Trees** ................................................... 43
   This Place Looks Familiar.............................................. 48
6. **Energy and Forces**..................................................... 51
   Perceptions and Emotions............................................. 62
7. **Scales of Balance**....................................................... 65
   The Secret to Contentment .......................................... 71
8. **Frustration Factor** .................................................... 75
   Peace is Necessary.......................................................... 81
9. **Who Are You?** ............................................................ 85
   Just a Little Difference Can Lead to Destiny............... 91
10. **Understanding Your Purpose** ................................. 95
    Outliers ......................................................................... 101
11. **The Harvest**............................................................. 105
    What Type of Sees are You Planting........................... 110
12. **It's All a Matter of Choice** ..................................... 113
    It's Okay to Spend Some Time Alone ........................ 120

**Conclusion**...................................................................123

# Acknowlegments

This book is dedicated to my wife, my children, my family and all of the people who have been instrumental in my spiritual, physical, emotional and intellectual growth.

To my wife, Cheree Clayton, who came into my life at a time that my individual strength was no longer sufficient for the battles that where ahead of me I want to say "I Love You" and thanks for all of your support. This book would not be possible without your unwavering belief in my dreams and your continued support.

To my children, I want to say thanks for being my first students and my first audience that were forced to listen to my theoretical approach on contemplation, critical thinking and choices.

A special thanks to all of my family, my extended family, my mother and father-in-law and my true friends. But a heartfelt special thanks goes out to my late mother and father whom I wished could have an opportunity to read my first book. Also, to my older siblings who were much older than me and never had the opportunities that I had. I truly believe in the concept that we are able to accomplish so much in life because we stand on the shoulders of those that paved the way. In John Salisbury's writings he wrote of Bernard of Chartres a medieval philosopher and theologian who used to compare us to dwarfs perched on the shoulders of giants. He pointed out that we see more and farther than our predecessors, not because we have keener vision or greater height, but because we are lifted up and borne aloft on their gigantic stature."

Every accomplishment I have ever had in life I always had a moment where I reflected on the sacrifices that others made that directly or indirectly benefited me and this time is no different.

So to everyone one who worked with me to ensure that this book made its way onto the shelves in bookstores, I want to say thank you, especially to my editorial team (Allwrite Communications); project manager (Rosemary Shedrick); proofreader (Cleary Stated Communications); and my graphic designer (Majesty Now Enterprises).

Last but not least, I want to say thank you to the Covenant Christian Center family and everyone else that I failed to make reference to or to mention. Please be assured that I'm a much better person, author, pastor, consultant and life coach as a result of just knowing you.

*-Thank You*

# Introduction

This book, "The Power of Your Choices," is not about being perfect or always making the right decisions. It is more about establishing a new way of thinking that affords you the opportunity to slow down enough to get off the treadmill called life to take some time to think about why you make the decisions that you make. This book encourages you to take more time to calculate your decisions and to weigh the benefits or consequences of every decision. This process is called contemplation. Contemplation is thoughtful or long consideration, observation, and spiritual meditation to invoke purpose or intention. In the game of chess, the object of the game is not to mimic the moves of the other player but to take your time to look at the entire chessboard. After careful contemplation, you then form a strategy and make your next move, which puts you in position to reach your goal.

In life, you should invoke this same strategy in your decision-making process if you want to get different results or change your old, destructive way of thinking. This strategy requires that you acquire rapid response-type decision-making skills. Such contemplation is a good tool to integrate into your life so that you can make decisions based on careful observation, your skill sets, and your true-life calling, or purpose.

Critical thinking is disciplined thinking that is clear, rational, open-minded, and informed by evidence. Critical thinking requires that you critique your decisions despite what is popular or how you have made past decisions. It is a process that takes into consideration the long-term benefits and consequences of each and every decision that you make. In simple terms, critical thinking is a process that looks beyond the surface of everything and takes into consideration the hidden things that lurk behind the smokescreen, looking deeper into a matter.

I like to look at critical thinking as "Iceberg Thinking" because the danger of an iceberg does not rest in the tip of the iceberg that is visible on top of the water; it lurks in the size of the iceberg that lies underneath the surface of the water. This reality was evident in the sinking of the RMS Titanic in April 1912. The Titanic was a state-of-the-art transatlantic vessel that was known as an "unsinkable" ship, and it was designed to be able to sail in the worst of conditions. The builders took into consideration the most difficult sailing conditions and inclement weather to ensure that this ship would not be in danger of sinking. However, they did not take into consideration human judgment or the role that critical thinking would play in the sinking of the unsinkable vessel.

The Titanic did not sink because it was flawed; it sank because of a simple error in judgment. I am not saying that the captain of the Titanic was the reason that the vessel sank. I am saying that the captain had no idea of the size of the iceberg that was lying underneath the water. Because he did not know the size of the iceberg, it was impossible for him to know how far to move away from it to ensure the vessel's safety; therefore, the ship hit the iceberg, and the rest is history.

In our own lives, we have to learn to look beyond the surface when we are making critical, life-changing decisions. The human mind has the ability to analyze, calculate, and arrive at a more objective conclusion based on reflection, contemplation, and critical thinking. Yes, we have the ability to make better decisions; we just have to learn how to take the time to use and rely on our intellectual, emotional, and spiritual abilities.

CHAPTER 1

# The Awakening

*Therefore, if any man be in Christ, he is a new creature: old things are passed away; behold, all things are become new.*

*~2 Corinthians 5:17 (KJV)*

It was a nice spring day in South Georgia at around 2:00 in the afternoon on March 27, 1997. I found myself staring at the ceiling, noticing things like stained tiles, chipped paint, and even some very old, rustic-looking light fixtures. There I was, just sitting there, pondering what the next few moments of my life would be like and reflecting on some of the decisions that I had made in my most recent past. Though I only sat there for only a brief moment in time, it seemed like hours, as time seemed to be moving in slow motion like in the Matrix. Also, to top things off, I was having an inward intimate moment replaying sound bites in my head of conversations that I had with people who were trying to encourage me to be more thoughtful about some of my decisions. I could hear the conversations loud and clear as if they were taking place right then and there; furthermore, to add fuel to an already burning fire, the very things some people had spoken to me about were unfolding right before my eyes.

I thought about my parents, family members, some of my teachers, Little League coaches, and numerous associates who came to me at different points in my life as if they had a glimpse into my future. There I was, sitting in a federal courthouse in Albany, Georgia. This moment sticks out so vividly in my mind because this was a kairos, or a defining moment, that would set the tone for the remainder of my life.

This was my moment, but we all will have a kairos moment at some point. For me, there was something about this moment, something alarming, something special, something captivating—as if this was my sink-or-swim moment, my last chance to get my life on track or I was going to die. Not that I was going to die physically, but it seemed like if I did not change my ways, I was going to drown spiritually and emotionally in my own stupidity.

As I sat there, I could have easily blamed my downfall on a list of other people, but this was my moment of truth. I had to stare myself right in the face. This moment was not about anyone else, but it had everything to do with the man in the mirror.

This moment appeared to be the end of something, but it was actually the beginning of something, an awakening. According to Dictionary.com, an awakening is the act of awaking from sleep, a recognition, realization, or coming into awareness of something. For me, it was as if I had been sleepwalking for years and now, in this moment, the alarm clock went off. I was suddenly awakened from a nightmare that had me doing things that no conscious person would ever do and making the type of decisions that brought me to Albany, Georgia, on this nice day in March 1997.

While sitting there, I heard the door opening, and I noticed two people walk through the door. I immediately recognized both of them: One was my attorney, and the other was the federal prosecutor. Before I could gather my thoughts, the door opened again, and a gentleman with a loud, booming voice said, "All rise!" It was the bailiff announcing the entrance of the judge who had been assigned to pass down a sentence upon me for money laundering and conspiracy to distribute an illegal substance.

Nothing in life would have prepared me for a powerless moment when it appeared that my future or destiny seemed to be in the hands of another person. My past decisions caused me to forfeit my rights to self-govern, so now my life and future were placed in the hands of someone who was not asleep at the wheel. The judge appeared to be a fair man with a non-anxious presence about himself, which allowed for me to be calm during this life-defining moment. Prior to passing down a sentence, he took the time to lecture me on the fact that he had read my pre-sentence investigation, which gave him some insight into what type of person I was prior to engaging in a criminal lifestyle. He scolded me for making selfish decisions, and then he uttered some words that still ring loudly in my ears. He said that I had potential and that he was going to give me an opportunity to get my life on the right track by departing from the established sentencing guidelines. For most people, the miracle would have been for me to get off scot-free, but that would have only enabled my sleepwalking ways. He sentenced me to 78 months in federal prison.

Even though I had just been sentenced, I left the courtroom that day feeling free and empowered because now, for the first time in my life, I was awake. I knew I was awake because everything was coming into focus, and now I had a renewed desire to make the most of every day, every moment, and every opportunity that presented itself to me. I encouraged myself not to see my period of incarceration as punishment but as a period of time to focus, study, learn, grow, and develop as a person. I am not going to glorify the prison experience as a much-needed vacation, but in my case, it was the hand that I was dealt because of my choices, so I made the best of a bad situation. For others, it may not be the threat of incarceration, but for each and every one of us, there is something that will play a vital role in helping us to awake from a deep sleep. The important thing is to recognize that moment and to use your moment of awareness to move your life in the direction that lines up with your God-given destiny.

For most of us, we think that the awakening starts with a

mental or intellectual consciousness, or maybe a renewed interest in taking care of our physical bodies. However, the awakening is much more than any mental or physical experience or transformation—it is spiritual. Therefore, to be awake, to be aware, and to have life starts with the spirit of life that was breathed into us in the very beginning. Prior to God breathing the breath of life into us we were simply existing in a physical form but without any form of life. That is how we will continue to function unless there is a renewed breath of life breathed into us that will give us a spiritual awakening.

I think that we can get a better understanding of this breath of life when we look closely at the creation story in the Bible. In Genesis 2:7 (NIV) the Bible says, *"Then the Lord God formed a man from the dust of the ground and breathed into his nostrils the breath of life, and the man became a living being."*

Prior to our spiritual awakening, we were not living, we were not awake, and we were not conscious. We were not capable of making the best decisions and recognizing divine opportunities. Instead, we were just going through the motions. Since we are creatures of habit and the brain is able to store experiences, we were able to do things that pertained to maintaining some level of functioning. But that pales in comparison to what we were created to do because we were just sleepwalking. The thing about sleepwalking is that we really don't know where we are going and what we are doing. Therefore, we are functioning in an unconscious state, placing ourselves at risk of harm without even being aware of any impending dangers. This sounds so familiar because this is how a great many of us live on a daily basis: sleepwalking and placing ourselves at risk of harm, making bad decisions, engaging in dangerous activities, hanging with the wrong crowd, and most of all, forfeiting our rights to live a balanced, fulfilling life.

In order to awake from our slumber, we must acknowledge, embrace, and establish a relationship with God the Father our creator, God the Son our redeemer, and God the Holy Spirit, which is our spiritual consciousness. It is in this relationship that we will become alert, awake, and spiritually conscious enough to recognize that there is more to us than we originally thought. We are God's creation, and we have been empowered to fulfill God's purpose while on this earth. We are to rule and have dominion or authority over all that God has placed in our care. Therefore, since most of us have been asleep at the wheel, I think that it is time for us to wake up and take our rightful place in our families, in our community, and in the world.

## A Clearer Picture

Our natural sight helps us navigate through our environment and plays a vital part in how we see life. But we have become so dependent on our natural sight that we make most of our key life decisions based on what we see in the natural world, neglecting other key factors. The amazing thing about totally relying on our natural sight is that we perceive what we have been conditioned to perceive, which makes our natural sight subjective at times.

There are times when two people look at the same thing at the same time, but they each interpret what they see differently. This happens because our past experiences influence what we see and how we interpret what we have seen. Since our natural sight is subjective, we must learn to develop and rely on something else when it comes to making key life decisions. We need something to help us see that "all that glitters is not gold." Likewise, we need something that will allow for us to see hope in a hopeless situation. Just think, one man's junk could be another man's treasure. It's all a matter of choice or in what you see.

In order to live life as you were destined, you must learn to trust your spiritual sight just as much as you trust your natural sight. Your spiritual sight gives you a clearer picture. I remember that before I was told I needed to wear eyeglasses, I thought that I was seeing pretty well. But things really came into focus when I put my glasses on for the first time. I could actually see a much a clearer picture.

Even though your natural eyes see that your life is in chaos, your spiritual eyes see that you are in transition. Therefore, it is not that things are so bad – it's just all in what you see.

The Bible says, *"We walk by faith and not by sight"* (2 Corinthians 5:7 NIV). Just remember, your faith will give you the spiritual sight necessary to see what your natural eyes could never see. You will have a clearer picture.

## CHALLENGE

What is something you are despairing about? What would common sense suggest that you do? What do your friends or family think you should do? Are you being led emotionally, mentally, socially or spiritually? Pray and ask God for wisdom and guidance. No matter how you feel, what you think or your peers may say, trust that He will direct your path toward His will and your best interests.

CHAPTER 2

# Like a Grasshopper

*"Jesus replied, 'What is impossible with man is possible with God.'"*

*~Luke 18:27 (NIV)*

What do you do when you are faced with gigantic life problems that invade your peace or upset the level of balance in your marriage, your family, your health, your career, your finances, or your relationship systems? We should all understand that there will come a time when you will receive a report informing you that giants have invaded your life and are trying to take possession of your land. In this moment, will you be paralyzed by fear, or will you continue to move forward in faith? When faced with this dilemma most of us operate out of fear instead of faith, causing most of us to see ourselves as grasshoppers instead of seeing ourselves as giant slayers. We spend more time reacting to the advances of the giants in our lives instead of moving forward with our life in spite of the circumstances. We actually start to develop the responder's mentality instead of operating out of an initiator's mindset. We wait for giants to make a move before we do anything. But if we are going to make it in this life and have any measure of success, we must learn how to move forward with the confidence of knowing that we are more than able to accomplish anything, especially when God is on our side.

In sports and in life, the most talented, the strongest, or the person with the largest supporting cast does not always win all the victories. Rather, in most cases, it simply boils down to each person's mindset. Contrary to popular belief, most victories or defeats take place long before the first pitch, pass, or play or before we walk in the room. Although physical conditioning is an important part preparing for a physical challenge such as a sporting event it is not the only aspect of preparation that will lead to success on the field. Most of us underestimate the value of mental preparation and spend the bulk of our time preparing physically and neglect mental preparation. Mental preparation is what separate winners from losers because it helps the winners achieve a focused, confident, and trusting mindset to help them compete at their highest level.

Tiger Woods changed the game of golf and made a mark in

the sport that could never be erased. During his early years on the PGA Tour, he developed what was known as the Tiger Effect: he was so mentally prepared for a tournament that he walked and carried himself as if he had already won the tournament before coming up to the first tee. And although Tiger is not playing competitive golf right now, you can still see the Tiger Effect every time another player walks up to the tee and stands behind the ball for a moment of mental preparation before striking the ball.

We should approach life the same way as Tiger Woods approached golf. We should be so mentally prepared that we see any obstacle as just a condition that is within our control and has nothing to do with our ability to be victorious or our potential level of success. Our approach to any situation should be the same regardless of the obstacle or the size of the opponent; you should never see yourself as a grasshopper or ascribe to what is known as grasshopper thinking

What is grasshopper thinking? Grasshopper thinking is when you have come to the conclusion that everything and everyone is bigger, smarter, and stronger than you are or will ever be in this lifetime. This type of mindset will cause you to settle for less, come up with every excuse for not being further in life, or justify and validate how you live your life. It will cause you to ascribe to the type of thinking that says that regardless of where you go and what you do, this is just how it is supposed to be for you. Ongoing mental preparation is one way to combat "grasshopper thinking," which is a gradual unfolding and part of a life-long process that grooms or prepares us to fail long before we take the field.

Yes, every word, every experience, and every relationship has groomed us to think the way that we currently think. It is our thought life or what is known as our dominant thoughts that lead to our actions and the adherence or neglect of some simple spiritual principles that will play themselves out in every area of our lives. Therefore, we should make no mistake about who we are because we are and always will be what we think that we are. But the bigger question for this moment is: How do we see ourselves: as giants or as grasshoppers? Because our lives are not determined by what others say about us or what they think about us, but more importantly by what we think about ourselves.

The Bible says, *"For as he thinks within himself, so he is. He says to you, 'Eat and drink!' But his heart is not with you"* (Proverbs 23:7 NASB). It is our own thoughts that will determine our outcome in life more than anything else. The amazing thing about this spiritual principle is that so many things in life are triggered or not triggered because of how we think or how we fail to think. Yes, our thoughts trigger a chain of reactions that will lead us to tap into our God-given talent, skills, and abilities, giving us a supernatural ability to do what we would not normally be able to do or accomplish. On the other hand, our negative thoughts will also trigger a chain reaction that will keep us paralyzed with fear, doubt, and unbelief so much that we never move beyond our self-imposed limitations and self-imposed prison walls. We will also be limited in every area of our lives; however, the sadder thing about these limitations is that we placed them on ourselves.

I think that it is important for us not to just focus on the end results of succeeding or failing. In order for us to better understand this process of thoughts, we have to go back to the beginning. There is an age-old controversy that has been argued in classrooms, churches, and think tanks for years: the nature vs. nurture debate.

Those who ascribe to the thought of the nature argument believe that your DNA is the sole or dominant factor in determining how you think, how you act, and where you ultimately end up in life. In other words, the cards are already in place to pre-determine how you will act and how you ultimately approach most situations in life; therefore, your upbringing and your foundational environments have little or nothing to do with how you act or think. I believe that our DNA plays a major part in the color of our eyes, the color of our hair, our height, our weight and our predisposition to certain health-related conditions, but in no way does it determine our thoughts and intentions. You can't change the color of your eyes or the color of your hair unless you subscribe to some man-made stuff like contact lens or hair color. However, you can change how you think, which leads me to the other side of the nature vs. nurture argument.

The nurture side of the debate leans more toward the environmental conditions that a person is born, raised, and educated in having the more dominant influence in how a person thinks, acts, and ultimately lives life. In other words, you replicate or act in a manner that lines up with how you have been taught intellectually and emotionally. This does not necessarily mean that you were instructed to do or not to do something, but it could have been subliminal or an unconscious type of learning that took place as a result of seeing something on a consistent basis. This is the same principle that is used in the education system of the United States, indicating that repetition and training can shape how a person thinks, acts and ultimately lives their life.

I tend to believe the nurture side of this debate because it lines up with the spiritual principles that I have come to embrace. It gives me, along with numerous other things, the hope that regardless of how we were raised, we can change how we think, act, and ultimately live our lives. The Bible gives me every indication that I can change how I think, act, and ultimately live.

*"And do not be conformed to this world, but be transformed by the renewing of your mind, so that you may prove what the will of God is, that which is good and acceptable and perfect."* Romans 12:2 NASB Version

It has been proven by neuroscientists that the human brain has the ability to change dominant thought patterns by reinforcing new experiences over a period of time. In other words, you can take a person who was raised, nurtured, and educated in a negative environment and place them in a different environment, thus introducing them to some new experiences. Over a period of time, this new environment leads them to think, act, and ultimately live differently. In no way am I saying that this will happen as a result of just being in a new environment, but I am saying that if a person puts forth an intentional effort to learn and change how he/she thinks, the human brain has the capacity to accommodate that type of change.

I have been aggressively working to change how I act, think, and ultimately live on a daily basis. Even though I have seen some results, I am encouraged to continue down this path so that I will not see myself as a grasshopper. Sometimes in life you have to look beyond your circumstances and take a closer look within because your problem is not that everyone is bigger, smarter, or stronger than you but that you see yourself as a grasshopper. It is also proven that others will replicate back to you what you are showing them. Therefore, if you see yourself as a grasshopper, others will see you that way as well. This is also a breeding ground for the victim mentality, where you blame everything and everyone for your place in life. You believe that it's the "white man's" fault, it's my father's fault, or it's the system that is designed to keep me down. No, it's not the "white man," your parents or the system. Rather, it's the man in the mirror – you.

One of the highest forms of deception does not take place in trusted relationships where someone betrays your trust or does something that breaks your heart. The highest form of deception takes place long before someone breaks your heart or betrays your trust. The highest form of deception is when you look in the mirror on a daily basis and convince yourself that you are not adequate, worthy, or smart enough, or you don't have the relationships or resources to move forward with your life. Therefore, the giants in your life don't have to do much to overtake you because you have already done most of the work for them.

In the Bible, there was a group of people who were destined to occupy a very rich parcel of land. But in order to get to the land, they had to go through a process that challenged and ultimately changed their old way of thinking. Numbers 13:30-33 records it, saying:

*"Then Caleb silenced the people before Moses and said, 'We should go up and take possession of the land, for we can certainly do it.' But the men who had gone up with him said, 'We can't attack those people; they are stronger than we are.' And they spread among the Israelites a bad report about the land they had explored. They said, 'The land we explored devours those living in it. All the people we saw there are of great size. We saw the Nephilim there (the descendants of Anak come from the Nephilim). We seemed like grasshoppers in our own eyes, and we looked the same to them.'"* (NIV)

This text of scripture is profound, and it is one of the foundational scriptures that I base my life upon. As a young boy, I was raised in an environment in which one of the greatest achievements was to just graduate from high school and get a good blue-collar job. Even though college was an option, it was only stressed to those who had the previous pedigree of going to college or to those whose family had the financial stability to support such a leap. This sort of lined up with the Booker T. Washington vs. W.E.B. Dubois debate. Booker T. Washington was occupied with the masses learning a trade that prepared them for a blue-collar job; on the other hand, W.E.B. Dubious said that, as a community, we should focus most of our resources on the "Talented Tenth." I'm glad that the African community did not adopt one of these arguments over the other because, when it's all said and done, it's more about the individual than anything else.

I neither came from a family with a pedigree for going to college nor did I come from a family that had the financial means to support me even if college was in my future. Therefore, my environment shaped my thoughts, my actions, and ultimately my life in such a way that I developed the grasshopper mentality. It was not until I was exposed to something else that I began to question my outlook on life. This is not an indictment against my relatives or the community of my upbringing because it was simply a way of life for most of us who grew up during that time.

The grasshopper mentality is not a death sentence—nor are you doomed to live a life of mediocrity—but it does reveal your past pattern of thinking. Therefore, to move beyond your past patterns of thinking you must be willing to do something different or experience something different even in the face of the criticism that will come and it will come. The funny thing about the criticism is that it is not just confined to your enemies. It will come from people who are close to you, from people who feel that you are disturbing the established structure or status quo, or from people who feel you are just trying to be different. Regardless of your critics or the level of criticism, keep moving forward with your life.

It is so easy to subscribe to the grasshopper mentality when it is the norm or when that is what you have been exposed to for the majority of your life. It is difficult to move beyond what has been the norm for so long because it seems so comfortable. On the other hand, you must be willing to take a leap of faith to activate or trigger a new way of thinking that will unleash who you really are and not who you have conformed to being. Underneath all of that fear, doubt, and uncertainty is another person inside of you who has been there all the time but never came to the forefront since the conditions were not conducive for growth. Therefore, even though you are a giant, you thought and conducted yourself like a grasshopper—that is, until today. From this day forward, all of your efforts, time, and energy should be directed at placing yourself in the right environment that will speak to who you were created to be.

Never underestimate the power of the right type of exposure and how it will impact your thoughts, your actions, and ultimately your life. I call it the "light bulb experience" because once the light comes on inside of your mind and you see and experience things that you have never seen before, it is hard to go back to that dark place again. Ralph Waldo Emerson said it best: "The mind, once stretched by a new idea, never returns to its original dimensions." This quote is an indication of how important it is to embrace change and new ideas. They trigger growth in the human mind, starting a chain reaction that begins to peel back the layers of doubt and fear and allowing for you to take a glimpse at the giant that lies within each and every one of us.

Therefore, just because someone is smarter, stronger, or has more resources than you does not mean that you should see yourself as a grasshopper. In fact, once you realize who you really are and have the corresponding actions to support your new thoughts, others will never see you as a grasshopper again but now they will see you as you see yourself, a giant.

### Running with Horses

As I watched the Kentucky Derby, I noticed that the horses were running at an alarming pace and that it seemed almost impossible for the other horses to compete with the winner. The best horse in show made a spectacle of the other horses, but each one of the competing horses had shown that they deserved to be in the race.

Life is a series of races in which we compete to work our way toward our destiny. However, life's race is not about winning or losing. It's more about having the guts to compete, having faith that you will finish, staying in your lane, and knowing that you have what it takes to be in the race in the first place. I know that you can run with men and women that look and act just like you, but the question is: Are you ready to run with the prize horses?

The biggest battles you will have to fight in life are the ones that will pull you out of your comfort zone. These battles will force you to run in races with people that are smarter than you, have more talent than you, and may even have more experience than you. Again, the question is: Are you ready to run with the prize horses? Each one of us has been blessed with phenomenal strength and ability to do great things, but most of us never get to that level because we faint at any sign of opposition. We give up during the small battles, not knowing that we possess the strength to overcome battles that are twice as big. The Bible says, *"If you have raced with men on foot and they have worn you out, how can you compete with horses?"* (Jeremiah 12:5)

## CHALLENGE

Spend some time thinking about what you will do at the next level because you will definitely get there if you keep practicing and just stay in the race. You will no longer be running against people who look and act like you. You will be running with prize horses, and there is no room for grasshoppers in a race for horses.

CHAPTER 3

# Road to Redemption

*"Do you not know that in a race all the runners run, but only one gets the prize? Run in such a way as to get the prize. Everyone who competes in the games goes into strict training. They do it to get a crown that will not last, but we do it to get a crown that will last forever."*

*~1 Corinthians 9:24-25 (NIV)*

Most movies, books, and documentaries have done a poor job of presenting rags-to-riches and personal redemption stories. Although some references are made about the difficult process of overcoming the odds and setbacks, most of the emphasis is placed on the trophy presentation or a positive storybook ending. Therefore, most of us love a good ol' comeback story, but what normally gets lost in the presentation of the comeback story is the numerous times that the story was almost never written. Also, for every good comeback story, there are hundreds of other stories where people were faced with similar situations and crumbled under the pressure.

The road to redemption story has become so commercialized that it has lost its human element. Therefore, most people feel like it is a given that anyone can bounce back from adversity and that the individual margin of error is erroneously large. This type of thinking has led a great deal of people down the wrong path of poor decision making.

The road less traveled is the road we take when we make better decisions. However, this only happens after we take the time to contemplate or when we take a long look at the long-term consequences or benefits that will accompany that choice. In other words, we treat this one decision as if it can have a drastic impact on our destiny. When faced with this type of dilemma, our overall well-being and our future are at stake. This is not the time to make an emotional decision or to make a decision based on what is popular. When facing a key life decision, we should treat it as if it is the most important decision of our lives. However, some of us think that we have the option of squandering precious moments because we will have time to get things right on the back end. Therefore, we place a lower emphasis on one of the greatest assets that a person can have: time.

Most of us approach life and key decisions so casually, and

we think that we have the latitude of time on our side. We tend to have the fun now mentality; we think we can do whatever we are big and bad enough to do with the hope that we can get things right when we get a little older. I am not trying to discourage anyone from having fun or telling anyone to be so serious all the time. However, it is important to know that redemption is not an event but a process, and it will take every ounce of our strength and focus to get our life back on track if it ever veers off course.

In order for personal redemption to take place, we must be willing to come to grips with the fact that in most cases the places that we are trying to redeem our lives from happened as a result of our personal choices. Therefore, it is going to require a greater level of discipline to get our life back on track than it would have if we had maintained our focus and made better decisions in the first place.

According to the scriptures, the principle of sowing and reaping is an ongoing process that will always give you back whatever you initially invested. It's a simple principle that is just as clear as the nose on your face, indicating that it is unrealistic to expect a return on something in which you never really invested. Genesis 8:22 says, "*As long as the earth remain there will be seedtime and harvest*" (NIV). This scripture is simply saying that planting seeds and reaping a harvest is an ongoing process that includes decision-making and it will never end. Therefore, how you live your life has a great deal to do with some of the situations that you find yourself dealing with at some point in your life. If only you had made better decisions in the first place, you would not have to be working so hard to get your life back on track. And the crazy thing about this whole process is the time and energy that you use to get your life back on track does not get you ahead. It simply gets you back to square one.

While writing this particular chapter I was involved in a process to get an exemption to participate in a federally funded program. It was through this exemption process that I realized that the road to redemption was not as glorious as it was made out to be through the over-dramatization by movies and books. And no matter how many obstacles I have been able to overcome in my life, there are always constant reminders that the residue of my past poor decision making was still playing itself out in my life. Even though I am years removed from some of my poor decisions, I am still forced to revisit my moments of blunder each and every day. As a result of my own blunders I thought it would be only fitting to emphasize two important factors that we should keep in mind: (1) the importance of maintaining our focus and the value of making good decisions, and (2) the overwhelming amount of energy, time, and effort required to get our life back on track.

In my travels and in conversations with people, I am often applauded for the great strides that I have made in working toward my own personal transformation. It is quite obvious that some work was required in order for me to accomplish some of the things that I have; however, I think that the level of sacrifice that was necessary actually gets lost in the accolades. It is the presentation of the trophy that attracts the most attention, but somehow the countless hours of hard work, toil, tears, and pain get lost and presented as simply a brief moment in time. That may be the case for the people who are watching from afar, but to the person who is actually doing the work, it seems like a never-ending process. A very influential person in my life once said that if his success appeared to be overnight, he truly does not want to experience another night like that one.

For most people, the amount of time, effort, and energy required to get their life back on track is normally double the amount of time that is necessary to maintain our focus initially. We also have to work twice as hard, but the benefits and rewards are the same.

The Book of Proverbs is full of nuggets and words of wisdom that were written as a guide to keep people from going down the wrong path. *"The proverbs of Solomon son of David. King of Israel; for attaining wisdom and discipline; for understanding words of insight; for acquiring a disciplined and prudent life, doing what is right and just and fair, for giving prudence to the simple, knowledge and discretion to the young; let the wise listen and add to their learning, and let the discerning get guidance for understanding proverbs and parables, the sayings and riddles of the wise. The fear of the Lord is the beginning of knowledge but fools despise wisdom and discipline."* Proverbs 1:1-7 NIV

This scripture really brought things into focus for me because it was not until I established a relationship with Jesus Christ that I was able to learn some personal discipline.

Although a good comeback story or someone's road to redemption story captures a greater audience, it is the application of knowledge, discipline, and wisdom that carries a greater value. Some people ascribe to the thought that knowledge is power, but I beg to differ because I know a great number of people who have a wealth of knowledge but who continue to make mistake after mistake. So for me, applied knowledge equates to power.

It is also important when discussing the road to redemption process to unpack the aspect and role of time. Time is one of the most underestimated assets in the world because no matter how hard you try you can never recapture time once it is used or lost. This concept became very clear to me while pursuing my MBA. During one of my classes I was introduced to what is called TVM, or the Time Value of Money concept. This concept indicates that money available at the present time is worth more than the same amount in the future because of its potential earning capacity right now. In essence, the value of the present time is greater than any time in the future.

If we could grasp this principle in our daily lives, we could empower ourselves even more by doing what is right in this present moment instead of waiting until our lives veer off course to get things right. Also, when we fail to maximize the moment, we underestimate the time needed to recover and be successful in any measure of personal redemption.

We should always remember that some mistakes can make

the road to redemption a short one. However, other mistakes can result in a road to redemption that lasts a lifetime. Lastly, in some cases the road to redemption may never fully come because the asset of time is so limited.

To the ones that have kept the faith, made good decisions, and stayed the course, I applaud your hard work and discipline. But for most of us, that is not our story. To the latter group, I want to encourage you to continue to work toward your personal transformation while walking down the road of redemption.

## Hostages of Past Kings

During the Old Testament period, the ascension of a new king to the throne was not a very smooth transition. It always presented a new set of challenges for the people — but even more of a challenge to the inner circle of the exiting king. This was certainly the case when the vision and ideology of the incoming king were different than those embraced by the old regime. To be most effective, the new king usually removed all members of the old king's inner circle from their key positions and held a ceremony for those people to publicly pledge an oath of allegiance to the new king. This was done to ensure that the future endeavors of the new regime would not be sabotaged because the people were still mentally, emotionally, and spiritually held hostage by past kings.

If we are to be honest with ourselves, most of us are being held hostage by past kings. We have moved into another city, career, church, or relationship, but we are still allowing our lives to be governed by people or things that played a significant role in our lives at another time. We are constantly sabotaging our future because we are still mentally, emotionally, and spiritually held hostage by past kings. This split allegiance is difficult because the very thing that holds us hostage was at one time relevant in our lives. Maybe someone gave you your first job, helped you during a difficult time in your life, loaned you some money, paid your way through college, or was your source of motivation. Does this mean that we should not be allowed to pursue a new life or our destiny because we are forever in their debt? No, we should always give honor to whom it's due and let the ones who were very instrumental in our life know how much we appreciate them but not to the point of being held hostage. Our life is a journey, and we will meet people along the way that will play a significant role in this process. However, we must keep these relationships in their proper prospective to maintain a healthy balance.

The Bible says, *"Cursed is the one who trusts in man, who depends on flesh for his strength and whose heart turns away from the Lord. He will be like a bush in wastelands; he will not see prosperity when it comes. He will dwell in the parched places of the desert, in a salt land where no-one lives. But blessed is the man who trusts in the Lord, whose confidence is in him."* Jeremiah 17:5-7 NIV

## CHALLENGE

Take some time to reflect on your life's journey to include the important people who have helped you along the way. If your allegiance to them is hindering or affecting your dreams, and you give them more credit than you do your true source of strength, you may be held hostage by past kings.

CHAPTER 4

# Ressurected Dreams

*"Then He said to me, 'Prophesy to these bones and say to them, "Dry bones, hear the word of the Lord! This is what the Sovereign Lord says to these bones: I will make breath enter you, and you will come to life. I will attach tendons to you and make flesh come upon you and cover you with skin; I will put breath in you, and you will come to life. Then you will know that I am the Lord."'*

*Ezekiel 37:4-6 (NIV)*

When the majority of us were young, our lives consisted mostly of doing things that brought a smile to our face. We spent a great deal of time dreaming or simply daydreaming. Life was filled with hope, and we spent a great deal of time thinking about the amazing possibilities of what could be in the not-so-distant future. Little boys living on a farm in the South had dreams of one day moving to California to surf the biggest waves and work as a computer analyst. Little girls living in the projects in a northern metropolitan city had dreams of moving down South to attend college and open a fashion boutique or a dance studio. Regardless of where the children lived and what their situations were at the time, most children had something in common: They all had dreams.

What is a dream, and why are dreams an important part of our spiritual, emotional, and intellectual life? A dream is a visionary creation of the imagination or a state of mind marked by abstraction or release from reality. Therefore, our dreams are creations in our minds that have the power to lead us to a place that does not physically exist at the present time. However, it does exist in our minds, which is the beginning stage of all things that man has been able to create or invent. It all simply started with a dream.

Sometimes as children of the most high God, we underestimate the awesome power of God or we are too quick to give up on something that God has promised. Instead of having childlike faith and holding onto our dreams, we settle into a routine and become carbon copies of the patterns that we have observed throughout the years. This type of mindset normally leads most of us to birth of a series of negative life-changing circumstances. Instead of us living a life filled with joy, happiness, peace, and prosperity, we become depressed, hopeless, and struggling based on the thoughts we allow to resonate in our heads and the words that we speak out of our mouths.

Because we trust in what we see with our physical eyes so

much, our sight determines how we process most situations in our life. And, based on what we see with our physical eyes, we tend to make final determinations or pronounce a status on our situations. Unlike when we were children when we dreamed in spite of our circumstances, we now focus more on our circumstances instead of focusing on our dreams. Therefore, the label or status that we place on our current situation is quite often the driving force for how we think, live, and ultimately speak.

I'm not trying to be unrealistic or super-spiritual and say that every dream will come true or everything in our lives is supposed to live forever. Because some dreams, relationships, and people that were a part of our lives in the past were already dead and should have been buried a long time ago. To be honest, some of the dreams, relationships, and people that are causing us so much pain right now should have been buried because they died long time ago, but we just extended the mourning period! We sometimes have a tendency to hold onto dreams, people, and relationships that were never destined to be a part of our lives or they have already served their purpose. But we continue to seek after things that make us happy instead of seeking after things that will lead us to our destiny. We seek after things that appeal to our selfish appetites, and we seek to establish relationships with people who fit into our limited physical world. This is mainly based on how they look, how they dress, or what they drive, not taking into consideration that they don't really fit into our destiny. This type of thinking is so shallow because it only focuses on the physical aspects while totally neglecting the spiritual, intellectual, and emotional values that a person may bring to the table.

Therefore, before we try to resurrect some of the dead things that were part of our lives, we should start the process of being more open and honest with ourselves. There are some things that were a part of our pasts that died, and they should remain dead to us because they pulled us away from our destiny and caused us to change the very nature of who we were created to be by God. How many times have we had to change what was right about ourselves to be able to sustain a relationship with someone? How many times have we had to make an unethical decision at work because our position demanded that we do so? How many times have we given in to the peer pressure of the moment and did things that altered our lives? If we have ever given in to any of these types of things, we may consider allowing for those things to remain buried because resurrecting them will only cause us to move further away from our place of purpose and destiny.

As we go through life sometimes we encounter situations that are so painful and draining that we ultimately give up on some of the things that are destined to be an important part of our lives. We lose hope and start another process that causes us to live beneath our skill sets and dreams. We actually start to settle for things that will lead us to live a life of mediocrity. Most of us have known people that we just knew they were going to be a success, have a great life, and do something major, only to see them years later and find out that they are only a fraction of the person that we thought they would become. How uncomfortable is that moment for us to know that the person that we saw so much potential in has settled for something far less than what we originally thought? I hate to say it, but this is the story for a great deal of people who are born with such great potential. It was once said that one of the richest places in the world is the graveyard because of the wealth of potential and resources that were never discovered or used.

What are some of the things in your life that you thought were dead and you had completely given up on? Some of us have given up on peace, joy, or happiness. We think that we will never experience happiness again because we have given up on the dream that God has given us. That dream could be to open a business; go back to school; buy a house; live a stress free life; or simply cultivate your God-given gifts, talents, and abilities. Because you have chosen to give up on your dream, you now exist as a fraction or crippled, limited version of who you were actually created to become. Sure, you go to work every day, you pay your bills, and you may even have some measure of success, but it all pales in comparison to what you were created to become. Now, complacency becomes the order of the day for you, and you establish this pseudo- success by getting into the same maze as the humans in the book Who Moved My Cheese? You drive to work the same way every day, you eat the same meal every Friday, you sit in the same pew at church, you go to the same barbershop at the same time every Saturday morning, and you go to bed at the same time every night. You are comfortable talking to people that look and act just like you, and anything that is a deviation from your boring structure turns your world upside down. Ultimately, after living like this for a while, your passion, motivation, and dreams slowly start to die like fruit on the vine that was never picked. A person who was once so full of life has now become like the Grinch who stole Christmas: bitter, unhappy, and unfulfilled. I like the Scripture that says, *"The thief cometh not but to steal and to kill and to destroy. I am come that they might have life, and that they might have it more abundantly."* (John 10:10 KJV)

The abundant life eludes most of us because we refuse to exercise spiritual principles that will change our lives and begin the process of resurrecting some of the things in our lives that we thought were dead. For most of us, living the abundant life can become reality if we simply started to dream again and start the process of resurrecting some of the dreams that we have allowed to die in our lives.

The term "resurrection" means the act of causing something that had ended or been forgotten or lost to exist again or to be used again. It is important for us to recognize that we have more power than we have been led to think that we have, especially when we use Godly spiritual principles to govern our lives. Often times, we overlook the power of words and the overall impact that our words have on our lives. Far too often we have assigned blame to other people and things that had little to no impact on our life circumstances. In those cases, we are simply just looking for someone to place the blame for our situation.

If you are looking for someone to blame for your unhappy life, you really don't have to venture out too far—just simply look at the man in the mirror. You may notice that he looks familiar. Actually, that person is very familiar, and it's you. Most of the time, we are our own worst enemies, and it normally starts with our words. Proverbs 18:21 says, *"The tongue has the power of life and death, and those who love it will eat its fruit"* (NIV).

I remember when we used to end church services by saying, "May the words of my mouth and the meditations of my heart be acceptable in thou sight O' Lord my strength and redeemer." How appropriate are these words when it comes to how we live out our daily lives? If our words are acceptable in the sight of God, they have the power to change and alter every one of our life circumstances. Words are very powerful, and they have the ability to take on a life form of their own once spoken into the air because they create the very circumstances that we uttered from our mouths.

Because our dreams are made of mental substances and imaginations that started in our own minds, there is no way that an outside force should be able to kill our dream. However, we allow for the forces of life to include any negative experiences to begin to form layers of doubt over our dreams to the point that our dreams are now buried in a tomb. And whenever we allow for our dreams to become buried under layers of the doubt we actually begin the process of dying a slow death. Yes, we are still breathing and doing the daily routines, but because we have lost hope of our dreams materializing we are simply just dead men walking. It is your dreams that keep you alive; it is your dreams that keep you motivated; it is your dreams that keeping you fighting; therefore, whenever you allow for the forces of life to cover up your dreams, you will soon die.

Because a dream is something that you birth from your own thought it is also something that you can resurrect. The question should not be whether your dreams can be resurrected but rather whether you are willing to put in the work to remove the layers of doubt. Without being aware of the impact of your words, you can say things that reinforce the layers of doubt instead of saying things that start the slow process of removing the layers so you can get excited about the possibilities of your dreams coming to pass.

There is a passage of scripture in the Bible that does an excellent job of conveying how we can start the process of resurrecting our dreams.

"The Lord took hold of me, and I was carried away by the Spirit of the Lord to a valley filled with bones.

2 He led me all around among the bones that covered the valley floor. They were scattered everywhere across the ground and were completely dried out.

3 Then he asked me, "Son of man, can these bones become living people again?"

"O Sovereign Lord," I replied, "you alone know the answer to that."

*4 Then he said to me, "Speak a prophetic message to these bones and say, 'Dry bones, listen to the word of the Lord!*

*5 This is what the Sovereign Lord says: Look! I am going to put breath into you and make you live again!*

*6 I will put flesh and muscles on you and cover you with skin. I will put breath into you, and you will come to life. Then you will know that I am the Lord.'"*

*7 So I spoke this message, just as he told me. Suddenly as I spoke, there was a rattling noise all across the valley. The bones of each body came together and attached themselves as complete skeletons.*

*8 Then as I watched, muscles and flesh formed over the bones. Then skin formed to cover their bodies, but they still had no breath in them"*

(Ezekiel 37:1-8 NIV)

We should always be mindful of the fact that our words have life in them. When we begin to speak words of life, motivation, excitement, and hope, our perspective about any situation will change. But more importantly, when we begin to speak to our dreams, nothing can hold them back to keep them from coming alive again. Therefore, it's time to get excited again about your future to the point that you begin to act like a child again, when you thought that anything was possible. Yes, it's time to dream again, because dreams can be resurrected.

## Hiding From Destiny

The path that the majority of us look for when embarking on the road to destiny is the one of least resistance. We have been led to think that we are on track for greatness when everything about our lives lines up into this orderly structure that goes from success to success. But as we peer through the window of history, we will notice that greatness and destiny rest right in the middle of the things that most of us are afraid to tackle. Instead of seeing the benefits of these challenges most of us procrastinate or get comfortable walking down the road of least resistance. We have learned how to sidestep life's defining challenges so well that we are now hiding from destiny.

Many of us have forfeited our right to greatness because we have settled for the comfort zone. We have placed so much emphasis on our material possessions, lifestyles, and reputations that we quake with fear when any of these things are threatened by change. So as we go to great lengths to protect our material possessions, lifestyle, and reputations we are actually hiding from our destiny.

The Bible says, *"This is what the Lord says – your Redeemer, the Holy One of Israel: 'I am the Lord your God, who teaches you what is best for you, who directs you in the way you should go. If only you had paid attention to my commands, your peace would have been like a river, your righteousness like the waves of the sea.'"* Isaiah 48:17-18 (New International Version)

## CHALLENGE

Take a few moments to look within to rediscover all of the things that you have allowed fear and procrastination to block. You just might realize that you have what it takes to overcome any obstacle and that your life has a specific purpose, especially when you are not hiding from destiny.

CHAPTER 5

# Forest for the Trees

*"But even if our gospel is veiled, it is veiled only to those who are perishing, among whom the god of this age has blinded the minds of those who do not believe so they would not see the light of the glorious gospel of Christ, who is the image of God."*

~2 Corinthians 4:3-4

Sight is one of the most important senses a person possesses. It is also one of the most neglected or misused senses as well. Most of us take for granted the fact that we have eyes but we do not clearly understand that most of our sight is limited to our perception, which is shaped by previous mental pictures of similar or past experiences. Therefore, instead of relying on our sight to truly see things for what they really are, we rely more on what things appear to be based on familiarity. Thus, we make bad decisions or jump to our own conclusions.

When we finally come to the place of recognizing that we have been destined to do great things, we should begin the process of taking an inventory of every aspect of our lives. We should also go through a process called reflection, in which we begin to look at the people and resources that we once had access to in our lives. At times, this process of recognition, inventory, and reflection can be earth-shattering or mind-boggling because it brings us face-to-face with an uncompromising truth.

As I was going through this process myself I noticed that one of the most obvious truths that I was forced to come to grips with is the fact that God would never destine for you to do something without making the necessary provisions available to you. Therefore, it is safe to say that God has placed everything that you will ever need in this life within your reach. At every junction of your life there awaits a full measure of resources to get you through the next season and ultimately on to your destiny. Actually, it's a fixed fight because everything has been orchestrated for you to make it to your place of destiny. However, it's important that you don't get so focused on the end results of your destiny that you forget to enjoy the full benefit of the lessons that you will learn along the way. Because every relationship, skill set, training, and experience that God allows into your life is going to work out for your good in the end. In the Book of Romans 8:28, this principle really comes alive:

*"And we know that in all things God works for the good of*

*those who love him, who have been called according to his purpose"* (Romans 8:28 NIV) This scripture gives us the assurance to know that despite what may be going on in our lives, everything is working out for our good and keeping us right on track to fulfill our God-given destiny. The awesome thing about destiny is that it is not something that is forced upon us because we all have a free will. However, if we really want it, it will happen. On the other hand, all of our life experiences, relationships, and decisions don't necessary lead us to a place of destiny. Some experiences, relationships, and decisions can lead us down a path that is detrimental to our well-being and ultimately doesn't work out for our overall good. This is one of the main reasons that I named this chapter, "Forest for the Trees."

Sometimes in life we go through a lot of unnecessary things because our sight and decision-making process need adjusting. Therefore, we see things that are not actually there or we fail to see or recognize things that are really there. Either way, we end up making poor decisions that sometimes cause us unnecessary pain. However, in order to walk in our God-given destiny, our sight must be adjusted so that we can see everything in its proper context. This sometimes can be a process within itself because our early life experiences and family experiences, such as how we were raised, along with societal projections, such as peer pressure, have caused our sight to get a little out of focus. Therefore, we see things as we have been trained to see things even though our eyes are wide open.

How many times have you made a decision based on what you thought you saw, and only after much reflection and review you went back and saw the same thing totally differently the second time around? This is a pattern that most of us repeat so often that we give up on ever having a meaningful life or being able to make good sound decisions. In most cases, the things that we need to make good life-changing decisions are there, but sometimes we just can't seem to see the forest for the trees.

In the Bible, there is a story that really brings this principle into context. One day, Jesus was going about the countryside teaching and healing people when he encountered a man who was totally blind. This man was absent of sight, but he wanted the ability to see. Jesus acted in accordance with what he had been called to do: give us life, and that more abundantly.

Let's look at the importance of our relationship with God and the importance of sight as written by Luke, one of the apostles chosen by Jesus:

*"The Spirit of the Lord is upon me, because he hath anointed me to preach the gospel to the poor; he hath sent me to heal the brokenhearted, to preach deliverance to the captives, and recovering of sight to the blind, to set at liberty them that are bruised"* (Luke 4:18 KJV).

We know that Jesus is all-powerful and there is nothing too hard for him. But as we examine this Bible story a little more closely, we will observe some things that I think are very powerful when it comes to the importance of our sight. The Gospel of Mark is a little more graphic, and he brings us face-to-face with the realities of having sight but still being in the need of focus.

"And He came to Bethsaida, and they brought a blind man unto Him, and besought Him to touch him.

And He took the blind man by the hand, and led him out of the town. And when He had spit on his eyes and put His hands upon him, He asked him if he saw anything.

And he looked up and said, 'I see men as trees, walking.'

After that He put His hands again upon his eyes and made him look up; and he was restored, and saw every man clearly."

(Mark 8:22-25 KJV)

Upon closer examination, we see that Jesus laid his hand on the eyes of the blind man so that his sight could be restored, but there is something interesting that happened that I believe we should take note of when we take into consideration our own sight. After Jesus prayed for the man and he received his sight, there was still a problem. Jesus asked the man, "What do you see?" The man replied, "I see men walking as trees." Just like the blind man, some of us have had our sight restored, but we still don't see things clearly. Rather, we see men walking as trees. We simply need another sight adjustment so that we can get focused.

Sometime we can't see the forest for the trees because we have gotten our sight back but things are still not in clear focus. So we get things right sometimes, but at other times we are way off, leading us back down a path of poor decision making. Some of us have really put forth the effort to change our views and perceptions of things, but because we operated in one mindset for so long, it is going to take a more intentional effort to bring things back into proper focus.

Earlier in this chapter, I mentioned the value of inventory and reflection and the role each will play in the process of adjusting your sight. As we work toward adjusting our sight, we should start the process of reflection, which will help us recognize some patterns, trends, and triggers that have led us to some of our past decisions. Time spent in the reflection process will also help us recognize similar things as they come into our view in the future and allow us time to revisit the consequences of our past decisions in that moment. As we continue to move forward to find a manageable balance in our lives we will also discover that our sight is an essential part of the decision-making process.

### This Place Looks Familiar

In July 1969, the United States moved beyond the established boundaries of gravity and landed on the moon. During that historical moment on television, astronaut Neil Armstrong stepped off the lunar spacecraft and spoke these words in a broken, static-filled transmission: "That was one small step for man, and one giant step for mankind." This event happened as a result of President John Kennedy's progressive thinking that we would go places where no man had gone before. It is so perplexing to know that we have been blessed with the ability to move beyond our self-imposed prison, but we insist on staying in the same old familiar place. We do the same things over and over again and we expect different results. But it's time for us to be honest with ourselves and say, "This place looks all too familiar."

We are creatures of habit; therefore, even though we know what the results will be in a situation, we still forge ahead. We find ourselves dating or marrying the same type of person who hurt us the last time; we end up in the same type of dead-end careers; we neglect to exercise and we eat foods that are bad for our health; and we are loyal to people that have shown us that they are selfish. We are frustrated and tired, but we continue to go back to that familiar place.

In this era, the people that we tend to look up to or those we deem successful are generally people that break away from established patterns and do something different. They move beyond boundaries and limitations to explore new frontiers or to go where no man has gone before. They get tired of going in circles only to find themselves back at that place of pain, rejection, and disappointment.

The Bibles says, *"Then we turned and took our journey into the wilderness by the way of the Red Sea, as the Lord directed me (Moses); and for many days we journeyed around Mount Seir. And the Lord spoke to me (Moses), saying, 'You have roamed around this mountain country long enough; turn northward.'"* (Deuteronomy 2:1-3 Amplified Version)

## CHALLENGE

Begin the process of breaking some of the engrained thought patterns that keep you going back to dead-end situations. In other words, move beyond your comfort zone and proceed in a different direction. Otherwise, you will look around and notice that this place looks familiar.

CHAPTER 6

# Energy and Forces

*"Verily, verily, I say unto you, He that believeth on me, the works that I do shall he do also; and greater works than these shall he do; because I go unto my Father."*

*~John 14:12 (KJV)*

During the few times in my life that I actually took a few moments to be reflective of where I came from, it became clear that my current place in life was not a coincidence or happenstance. Instead, it was a clearly defined pattern of how I used or handled the energy and life forces that were within my grasp that shaped my life more than anything. There were times when I was a wise steward of my energy and life forces, but there were other times when I squandered my time, energy, and life forces. The latter dominated most of my time, energy, and life forces; therefore, I spent a large part of my life living beneath my abilities and destiny.

What are energy and life forces, and how do they play out in our lives on a daily basis? How do they affect our destiny or level of personal successes, whether spiritual, financial, or relational? Energy is defined as the capacity for working or acting; a vigor, strength or force. And force is defined as an energy or strength, power, an intellectual influence to inflict or impose one's will.

As we can see in the definition of these two words, there is enough evidence to indicate that our energy level has a limited capacity and that force is a direct product of our will. All we have to do is take the time to consider how energy and force play out in our daily lives, and we will notice that our energy level is not limitless; therefore, we must be more mindful of how we use our energy. Because we have not seriously taken into consideration the impact of the misuse of our individual resources, we have not been wise stewards of our limited energy capacity. This has led most of us to deplete our energy reserves and not have an adequate amount of energy or life force to direct us toward the things that will produce favorable results in our daily lives.

Most of us have not taken into consideration the amount of energy we invest in people and negative activities on a daily basis; therefore, we don't understand the reason for our current state or condition. We simply have underestimated the value of our personal energy level and the important role it plays in how we are able to successfully navigate through life on a daily basis.

Have you ever thought about how much of your personal energy you use daily talking on your cell phone, gossiping, hanging out, watching meaningless television programs, interacting with negative people, participating in sibling rivalry, and dealing with relationship problems? Most of these activities lead to stress, anxiety, and depression, all of which can aggressively deplete your personal energy capacity. If we were to be honest with ourselves, we can admit how drained we feel after being engaged in any of the above-mentioned activities. They deplete you of your positive creative energy, and the more of your energy and life forces you direct toward negative things, the less energy you have to direct toward things that will produce success.

The majority of us underestimate the value of our personal energy so badly that we try to circumvent wise stewardship and personal discipline with prayer and faith principles. We actually believe that we can live an undisciplined life and use prayer and faith as a last-minute attempt to get good results. I strongly believe in prayer, faith, and spiritual principles, and I have incorporated both into my daily life. But I also know that I must balance out my prayer and faith with a work ethic that is centered on those same Biblical and spiritual principles. The Bible talks about people who rely upon their faith without applying any work or without maintaining enough discipline to see the results of their faith: *"What doth it profit, my brethren though a man say he hath faith, and have not works? Can faith save him?"* (James 2:14 NIV).
Faith is a necessary component that we must have in order to have

any measure of success in our daily lives and it is safe to say that without it, our hopes would be dashed. However, we also must begin to live our lives in a more balanced manner.

We are living in a time in which the benefits of modern technology and the well-calculated plans of marketing executives have caused most of us to be lulled to sleep. We have actually adopted the instant recovery mindset. We don't see the need to maintain a disciplined lifestyle because whenever things spiral out of control we believe we can instantly get them back on track. It's called the microwave mentality. The microwave oven is a good appliance to have in the home, but today many parents don't plan meals anymore because the benefits of this modern technology allows them to come home at 7:00 p.m. and have dinner ready by 7:30 p.m. This microwave mentality is the same approach that most of us take toward how we live our daily lives. It seems like we can instantly recover from lost family time by simply rushing into the home and still having dinner on the table by 7:30 p.m. What we miss through this process is the value of being a better steward of our time through proper planning, spending quality time with our spouse and children, and eating food that is healthier for our bodies.

One of the consequences of this type of thinking is evident in our spiritual lives. We have taken this type of approach toward life and incorporated it into our relationship with God, the church, and our overall spiritual walk. We actually believe that we can live an undisciplined life, not plan for our future, spend endless hours being idle, never develop our skills and talents, never try to cultivate productive meaningful relationships, never spend the proper time building a strong relationship with God and yet expect one prayer to correct our current situations. This is one of the greatest deceptions, and it has led most of us to become too reliant on one individual in the church community to keep us connected to God. This happens all over this country on Sunday mornings because we are too undisciplined to spend time with God ourselves. It is good to remember that instant gratification normally leads to a belief system that undermines discipline, hard work, and dedication.

I think that most adults can relate to simple situations we encounter with our children to help us better understand that we need to begin to live a more balanced life. Suppose your son or daughter is getting ready to take a college entrance exam, but on the days leading up to the exam, they are texting their friends, posting on Facebook or watching their favorite television show. At some point you will become a little concerned and ask your child if they think they are going to pass the exam. Their reply is a simple and straight to the point, "I got this." As a parent myself, I see your blood beginning to boil. You actually have to contain yourself to keep from losing your religion. I know the feeling because it appears that your child has squandered most of their energy on meaningless activities, yet they expect to walk into the exam and master the test. That's the same way most of us approach our daily lives, but yet we expect to be successful and live a balanced life.

If we want to experience any measure of success in our daily lives, we must begin the process of practicing balance. It is sad to say, but most of our life energy and forces are used on maintaining negative relationships or participating in negative activities. Hanging out with friends, watching television, and talking on the cell phone are not inherently negative activities. But if these activities are dominating the majority of our days, then we are exerting too much of our life energy on them, and they then become negative activities.

Everything in life that works properly operates in a balance, or a homeostasis. According to dictionary.com, the term homeostasis simply means "a state of equilibrium between different but interrelated functions or elements." This means that a proper amount of our time, effort, and energy is necessary in everything we do if we want to experience any measure of success. I will expound more on the importance of balance later in this book.

I think we can learn a valuable life lesson from the Bible, which indicates: "There is a time and season for everything under the sun. There is a time for everything, and a season for every activity under the heavens: *a time to be born and a time to die, a time to plant and a time to uproot, a time to kill and a time to heal, a time to tear down and a time to build.*" (Ecclesiastes 3:1-3 NIV)

Because so many of us are acting out-of-balance, it seems normal for us to spend most of our life energy on negative activities. One of the ways people deplete most of their life energy is maintaining negative relationships, or being unequally yoked—

spending time with people whose vision, perceptions, preferences, and goals don't align with ours. We spend a great deal of our life energy in close relationships with people who are either codependent or enablers. Codependency is a type of dysfunctional helping relationship where one person indirectly supports another person's drug addiction, alcoholism, gambling addiction, immaturity, irresponsibility, or under-achievement. Codependent people are people that have invested themselves in people who rescue them, or someone that who is over-dependant on others for emotional, spiritual, physical or financial assistance. On the other hand, an enabler is someone that we become dependent upon, and they become our source of strength, guidance, or support. No matter the extent of dependency, the relationship system is out of balance and causes both individuals to function below average or not live up to their full potential. The Bible has several examples that we can use as a guide on how we should govern ourselves in relationships: (1) "Can two walk together, except they be agreed?" (Amos 3:2 KJV); and (2) "Iron sharpeneth iron; so a man sharpeneth the countenance of his friend" (Proverbs 27:17 KJV). It is important for us to always remember that our relationship systems must be balanced if we are going to live a fulfilled life.

It is vitally important that we don't go to any extremes in this area of our life. Therefore, I am not encouraging anyone to disconnect from people because they may be negative at times or because they are not on the same page with us in everything that we do or say. I am simply saying that we should be aware, conscious, or more guarded of the amount of time we are dedicating to these types of relationships. This type of approach should also include our family members who use their position in the family to justify their negative presence in our lives. By virtue of DNA we will forever be connected to our relatives, and we should make every effort to enhance those relationships—but not at the expense of destroying our own lives. Having the same DNA or bloodline is not a valid excuse for us to be content acting out of balance or expending most of our life energy on under-functioning people, even if they are our relatives.

Most of us are enablers to under-functioning family members, and we hurt them more than we help them. As long as we continue to act out-of-balance in key family relationships, we are creating a negative atmosphere that will continue throughout generations to come. I think that it is time for us to move beyond some of our deeply engrained family relationship patterns and start operating in a more objective manner. Some of us are even held hostage to promises that we made to our parents concerning some of our relatives. Does this sound familiar? "I told mom before she died that as long as I am alive I will look after June, my younger brother." But your younger brother has no interest in growing up or accepting responsibility for his actions, and he is lazy and careless with money. Does this mean that you should continue to use your hard-earned resources to continue to rescue him every time he has a problem?

The best way to navigate through life successfully is to develop a set of guiding principles that we can use in any relationship, including family members. Also, it is vitally necessary for us to be more conscious of the amount of our life energy we dedicate to anything, such as activities and relationships, so that we are focused enough to accomplish our own personal goals. It is important for us to become more consistent in applying these guiding principles to our daily life if we want those around us to make the proper life adjustments based on our consistent life style.

As we learn to become better stewards of how we apply our life energy on a daily basis, we will begin to notice that our level of stress, depression, and anxiety will decrease, putting us into a more peaceful mindset. And this peaceful state of mind will allow for us to be more in tune with God, our divine purpose, while putting us in a position to focus more of our attention and energy on the things that can change our lives and lead to a more balanced and successful lifestyle. Contrary to what most of us have been led to think, there is no human being other than ourselves who has the power to hold us back in life, including our boss, family, friends, and worst enemy. No one has the power to hold us back or make our lives miserable. The power is in our own hands, and we have to decide how we are going to use our life energy and life forces on a daily basis.

I remember sitting in church during the offering portion of the service noticing that most leaders were trying to convince the parishioner that giving 10 percent of their income should be an easy thing to do, especially since God was the one responsible for their blessings. My initial thoughts were that you should not have to encourage people to do what was right in the first place. But as I gave more thought to this dilemma, I walked away looking beyond the surface. In my moment of deeper reflection, I concluded that people don't give less because they don't love God or they don't want to support the church. The reason can be as simple as most people never take the time to do a financial inventory to really see where their financial resources are used. A simple financial inventory of a person's spending habits would help them to be more aware that their spending was out of balance. It is a challenge giving God what rightfully belongs to him if a person is using their resources improperly and living an undisciplined lifestyle.

This is the same approach we need to take if we are going to get our lives back into balance. We need to take a personal inventory of our total lives, including our relationship system and activities, to see where most of our personal energy and life forces are being directed. Our days consist of only 24 hours, so if we are going to change some of our bad habits we must know what we are doing with every minute of our day. Start keeping a daily journal that begins each day when you get up in the morning. The use of smartphones and computers have made this task easy. You can document what you are doing with your time to include how much time you sleep, watch television, talk on the phone, drive to work, read, pray, etc. Do this exercise for 30 days, and at the end of the 30-day period, calculate how much time you are dedicating to each activity. You are going to be surprised what you are using the majority of your time, energy, and life forces doing.

This simple exercise will allow for you to better understand your current place in life and what you need to do to bring more balance into your life. If your family is falling apart, maybe you are spending too much time at work, the gym, or just hanging out with the boys. Maybe your house is not clean because when you are not working you are spending 6-8 hours of the day on your cell phone or on the computer. Regardless what activity you are spending the most time doing, spending too much time on just one thing will cause a lack or deficit in other areas of your life.

I am not advocating that you become so serious that you don't take time to stop and smell the roses as you go through life. Rather, I am simply trying to raise your level of awareness about some of the things we overlook in our daily lives. We have millions of cells in our brain, but we have become so repetitious that we only use only a portion of our intellectual ability, causing us to operate at a level far below what we were created do to. As we increase our level of awareness, it is this type of thinking that can revolutionize a generation and break the vicious cycles that have existed in most of our families as long as we can remember. It is time for us to move beyond the trivial things and stop equating success with materialism because true success is in knowing how to appropriately use your personal energy and life forces. If we learn how to properly use our energy and life forces, we will begin to walk and operate at a level in which we will reach our goals and ultimately live a more balanced and purposed filled life.

## Perceptions and Emotions

During the 1990s, there was an explosion of late-night infomercials that appealed to our emotions with hopes of getting us to buy things that we really did not need. We were bombarded with everything from instant weight loss formulas, to things that would make you rich overnight or ways to get a college degree in 30 days. Marketing professionals have learned that we make spur of the moment decisions, especially when they appeal to our emotional side.

Two of the things that have caused us to error in our judgment more than anything are our perceptions and our emotions. We pay more attention to our feelings and our assumptions about something than we do to objective facts. These errors in judgment have caused us to compromise our decision making when the truth is staring us right in the face. We see the writing on the wall, but somehow we think that it will all be okay if we think positive about a situation. We know that the relationship is not good for us; we know that bad spending habits lead to poverty; we know that if we stay out all night it will affect our performance at work; and finally we know if you never change our eating habits it will probably lead to poor health.

Making emotional decisions are not just confined to our spending habits but it also to how we enter and exit relationships, how we choose careers and even how we worship. Regardless of which arena you are operating in, you must make more thoughtful decisions unless you are willing to accept the consequences that accompany emotional decisions. It's time for us to stop blaming the devil, our enemies, or our friends, and start placing the blame where it really belongs. The Bible says, *"For those who live according to the flesh set their minds on the things of the flesh, but those who live according to the Spirit, the things of the Spirit. For to be carnally minded is death, but to be spiritually minded is life and peace."* Romans 7:5-6 (NKJV)

## CHALLENGE

Spend some time looking at how you have made decisions in the past and you just might notice that it was not your best thinking. Instead, it was your perceptions and your emotions that determined your choices.

CHAPTER 7

# Scales of Balance

*"But the fruit of the Spirit is love, joy, peace, longsuffering, gentleness, goodness, faith, Meekness, temperance: against such there is no law."*

*Galatians 5:22-23 (KJV)*

In times past, one of the best ways to ensure that a fair exchange took place between two individuals who were entering into a business transaction included some type of measurement, weight, and use of a scale. In the transaction, the item at the center of the business deal was placed on a scale. The weights were adjusted to ensure that the amount of the item that was requested was in alignment with the weights on the opposite end of the scale, ensuring equity and fairness for both parties. This process was known as balancing. Balance is something that we often talk about but spend very little time trying to create in our own lives.

Living a life of balance is so important that we can never reach our full potential unless we learn to discipline ourselves to function in some type of balance. It is vitally important that we find a way to establish some level of equilibrium in our lives or we will forever be wasting our time, energy, and focus on an unrealistic attempt to reach our destiny. Over the last 20 years, there has been a mental shift that has most of us thinking that we can live undisciplined and unbalanced lives yet still reach our destiny. We have been led to think that being successful, reaching our goals, or living a fulfilled life is an effortless process. Some of us even try to randomly use positive thinking faith principles as a substitute for establishing some level of balance in our lives.

The Bible is very clear and sends a strong message that indicates that in order to attain any level of success or to reach our full potential we must be willing to balance out our faith with a corresponding level of action. This is really noticeable in religious circles where people try to forge ahead in faith without putting forth any positive effort. The Gospel of James acknowledged this dilemma in James chapter 2.

*"What good is it, my brothers and sisters, if someone claims to have faith but has no deeds? Can such faith save them?*

*15. Suppose a brother or a sister is without clothes and daily food.*

*16. If one of you says to them, 'Go in peace; keep warm and* well fed,' but does nothing about their physical needs, what good is it?

17. In the same way, faith by itself, if it is not accompanied by action, is dead.

18. But someone will say, 'You have faith; I have deeds.'

Show me your faith without deeds, and I will show you my faith by my deeds.

19. You believe that there is one God. Good! Even the demons believe that—and shudder.

20. You foolish person, do you want evidence that faith without deeds is useless?

21. Was not our father Abraham considered righteous for what he did when he offered his son Isaac on the altar?

22. You see that his faith and his actions were working together, and his faith was made complete by what he did.

23. And the scripture was fulfilled that says, 'Abraham believed God, and it was credited to him as righteousness,' and he was called God's friend.

24. You see that a person is considered righteous by what they do and not by faith alone.

25. In the same way, was not even Rahab the prostitute considered righteous for what she did when she gave lodging to the spies and sent them off in a different direction?

26. As the body without the spirit is dead, so faith without deeds is dead"

(James 2:14-26 NIV).

Most of us live our daily lives thinking that there is some type of magical pill, software, or new fad that will miraculously make up for our lack of discipline and balance. Therefore, we waste precious time thinking that whatever time is lost due to a lack of balance can be recouped in a matter of minutes, days, or weeks.

Some of us are great thinkers. Some of us have great physical abilities. Others are very much in tune with our spirituality. These are the areas that some of us seem to excel in more so than others, and that is not a problem. The problem starts when we begin to neglect the other areas of our lives because we don't operate in the other areas at a high level. It is a natural inclination to gravitate toward the things that we do well, but the more emphasis we place on our areas of strength the less attention we give to improving in our areas of weaknesses. I am not advocating for anyone to downplay their strengths, but whenever we pay too much attention in one area at the expense of neglecting other areas, we become unbalanced.

The Bible contains a great number of scriptures related to remaining balanced and avoiding all forms of extreme and one that seems to capture my thought on this matter is found in the Book of Ecclesiastes:

*"In this meaningless life of mine I have seen both of these: the righteous perishing in their righteousness, and the wicked living long in their wickedness. Do not be over righteous, neither be overwise—why destroy yourself? Do not be overwicked, and*

*do not be a fool—why die before your time? It is good to grasp the one and not let go of the other. Whoever fears God will avoid all extremes. Wisdom makes one wise person more powerful than ten rulers in a city"* (7:15-19 NIV).

Whenever we neglect any part of our core being (mind, body, and spirit), we get out of balance, and that can lead to a lot of unhealthy decisions, activities, and relationships. One of the things that come to mind when we talk about being out of balance is the numerous times we enter into unhealthy relationships because we are looking for another human being to do for us what we have neglected to do for ourselves. We spend numerous years looking for someone to complete us or to give us that balance that is missing from our lives. News flash: No human being can complete us or fill the voids in our lives. People can enhance who we are, but God is the only one that can complete us or cause us to function as He created us to function and fill those voids in our lives.

Everything that God made was created to function in harmony with other things He created so that the earth would function in an orchestrated balance. Genesis 8:22 says, *"As long as the earth remains seedtime and harvest, cold and heat, summer and winter, day and night will never cease"* (NIV). This particular scripture is a good indication of the importance of balance when something is designed to operate in a structured order.

The earth is constantly teaching us valuable lessons about

how important balance is in everything. Depending on what season we are in, the sun will produce a certain number of hours of daylight as the earth rotates on its axis. This is not a coincidence but by design; too many hours of daylight would cause plants and vegetation to die and rivers to dry up. This would create a level of chaos that would eventually cause the whole ecosystem to spiral out of balance.

Too much of one thing and not enough of another will always lead to problems in our lives as well. Just as the earth was created to operate in balance, we were created to operate in balance. And whenever we don't operate in our created balance, we can trace back every problem we have encountered in life to operating out of balance in one or more areas.

Man was created in the image of God, and He blessed us with everything we will ever need to function in accordance with our destiny. We were created with a body, soul, and spirit, and each area of our core being is designed to function in harmony with the others. Most problems that we encounter are not manufacture defects; they are problems that can be traced back to a lack of discipline, structure, and balance in one or more areas of our lives.

Some of us spend a great deal of time working on our physical body or appearance. We work out, go on all types of diets, have plastic surgery, or add hair, all for the sake of making sure that our physical body looks and functions at its maximum potential. This is a good thing; however, whenever we don't place the same level of discipline and dedication to our soul and spirit, we are physically strong but intellectually and spiritually weak. The Bible speaks on the importance of bodily exercise or about the benefits of taking care of our physical body. However, it also states that if bodily exercise is our only pursuit, it will only profit or benefit us a little. *"Have nothing to do with godless myths and old wives' tales; rather, train yourself to be godly. For physical training is of some value, but godliness has value for all things, holding promise for both the present life and the life to come"* (1 Timothy 4:7-8 NIV).

Physical improvements have their benefits, but we should also be willing to invest the same amount of time to all of the other areas of our life so that we do not become one-dimensional. Whenever we are out of balance, we are out of sync, and whenever we are out of sync, we miss out on something called "synergy." What is synergy? It is simply the interaction of two or more agents or forces where their combined effect is greater than the sum of their individual effects. So as we can see we become more focused, stronger, and wiser when we have a synergetic flow and everything in our lives is working in harmony with each other so that we can live a more balanced life.

## The Secret to Contentment

We live in a world in which our thinking is bombarded daily by a well-planned marketing attempt to get us to the latest fades in technology, in fashions, automobiles, weight loss products, and furnishings for our homes. We have become so materialistic that companies spend billions of dollars each year to ensure that they come up with the right jingle, slogan, or commercial marketing that tells us that we must have this product or service. Marketers know that the atmosphere is right and they have created a society in which most people are more concerned about what they wear, where they live and what they drive than how they think and how they live.

Anxiety is at an all-time high, people are working multiple jobs, children rarely spend quality time with their parents, sleep deprivation is almost the norm, and people are now equating spirituality with material possessions. How did we get here? We simply lost our focus and started to focus more on the gifts than on the one who was blessing us with the gifts.

It is important to remember that you are not defined by what you wear, where you live, or what you drive, but you are defined by the quality of your relationship with God and with each other. There are so many people that have great material possessions, but they are lonely, hard to get along with and live unfulfilled lives. There is a certain contentment that comes from having a quality relationship with God that will sustain you whether you have plenty or just a little, and it will help temper your crazy desires to seek after all of the latest fads. It is okay to have and enjoy the finer things in life, but the secret to contentment is to establish a balance. That can only come from God.

The Bible says, *"I know what it is to be in need, and I know what it is to have plenty. I have learned the secret of being content in any and every situation, whether well fed or hungry, whether living in plenty or in want. I can do all things through Christ who gives me strength."* Philippians 4:12-13 NIV.

## CHALLENGE

Spend some time thinking about what really defines you and how you can create a balance in your life. Thus, when you will find the secret of contentment.

CHAPTER 8

# The Frustration Factor

*"Then the people of the land discouraged the people of Judah, and frightened them from building, and hired counselors against them to frustrate their counsel all the days of Cyrus king of Persia, even until the reign of Darius king of Persia."*

*Ezra 4: 4-5 (NIV)*

One of the common themes that I hear from a great number of people who have overcome great odds but yet persevered on to do something great is that at some point of their journey they felt overwhelmed or they got frustrated. It seems like at some point in everyone's life, we all will have to learn how to overcome the emotional state of being frustrated or discouraged and continue to work toward our destiny or even short-term goals. Based on this observation, it would be safe for me to say that the "frustration factor" is woven into the fabric of any measure of success. If we want to experience success, we must be prepared to deal with some level of frustration along the way.

In order to be successful at anything you do in life, you must sit down and calculate the cost of what it is going to take to finish the project, reach a goal, lose weight, finish college, start a business, have a successful marriage, become a better person, or simply get good results in every area of your life. Even though this may sound elementary, you would be surprised at the number of people who take a leap of blind faith without ever taking into consideration the unforeseen circumstances that could potentially happen along the way. I am not trying to discourage you from trying to reach your goals. Rather, I am suggesting that you must learn how to balance out faith and works. *"Suppose one of you wants to build a tower. Won't you first sit down and estimate the cost to see if you have enough money to complete it?"* (Luke 14:28 NIV)

The planning stage of any endeavor is vitally important because it brings into account the number of resources that are necessary to complete a project. As I travel, I am amazed at the number of unfinished building projects I see that started out with great intentions but somewhere along the way were aborted because of a lack of resources or failure to overcome some other degree of challenges. Whether it was poor planning, a lack of resources, or the inability to endure through the frustration or challenges; without properly planning most projects are not completed. What about you? How many projects have you started and then aborted somewhere along the way even though you knew they would change your life for the better? Probably too many to count. But that's not important, because regardless of the number of challenges that you have faced in life, you can regroup and overcome them all if you learn how to cope, deal, and overcome your frustrations.

Anyone who wants to experience any measure of success must also develop some coping skills to deal with the unforeseen situations that may occur. If success was easy, then more people would experience a higher level of success; but the truth is that success is not easy. Most people think that a lack of resources is the primary reason that only a few people experience a high level of success, but I beg to differ. I am in no way underestimating the role that a lack of resources can play in a person's life, but I am also aware of the importance of developing the necessary coping skills to help navigate through any form of opposition that people may encounter.

There is one important factor that the majority of us fail to take into consideration when we are working toward our goals or trying to attain any measure of success: the frustration factor. The frustration factor is when you reach a point in your endeavor when none of the circumstances align themselves with our vision or we are experiencing some unforeseen circumstance that is hindering our progress. The funny thing is that although the lack of resources can be a factor, the majority of our problems come from the discouragement or negative words of those we have allowed to play some role in our lives. This role does not have to be significant to impact us in a very negative way. The people that we surround ourselves with while working toward our goals can influence how we deal with crisis or setbacks. I am not saying that everyone has to agree with our vision or goals; however, it is very important to surround ourselves with people who clearly understand that dreams can come true with the right resources and relationships.

We must maintain a high level of balance in everything that we do in life if we are going to be successful. Therefore, once we have done our due diligence, counted up the cost, and positioned ourselves to take the necessary steps towards reaching our goals, we must brace ourselves for some turbulence. It is during the storms, turbulence, and setbacks that the words of the people who are closer to us will encourage us to keep moving forward or discourage us and cause us to throw in the towel.

The way we navigate through the frustration factor will have a direct impact on whether we reach our goals or simply become another statistic. Life does not stop happening because you decided to move forward, make better choices or we woke up with a renewed interest in reaching our life goals. Life will continue to unfold, and you will continue to encounter negative forces that are designed to frustrate your purposes. A negative force or influence could be something that is very obvious or it could come in the form of something that looks well meaning. Obvious negative forces are things that are clearly seen as determinates to your success and include depression, stress, negative peer association, alcoholism, or substance abuse. However, some negative forces or influences are not as obvious but they affect your life in the same manner as the obvious negative forces.

There are two negative influences that get very little attention because they come disguised in the form of relationships. One is that we sometimes allow for people to occupy so much space in our lives that we either take on things that don't belong to us or we over-invest in them, leaving very little energy or time to pursue our own goals. Time is the other influence that we pay little attention to because we have this mindset that it is an unlimited resource when in reality it is not. Time is one of our most limited resources that we have at our disposal, and until we begin to treat time as an asset, our time will work against us instead of working on our behalf. Whenever we allow for any type of negative force to dominate our efforts to change or move closer to our destiny it frustrates our purpose and at times cause one to become inconsistent or give up on their efforts all together. Whenever we don't factor in the impact of negative influences or factors we can easily become a person who starts something but does not factor in everything that is necessary to complete the endeavor.

The frustration factor can also be seen as a deterrent to our success, but it depends on how we look at it—it can also be a blessing as well. It is important to develop coping skills to combat the frustration factor because when the frustration factor manifests itself, it attacks our faith, patience, hope, and focus. So, instead of spending our time and energy on reaching our goals, most of us go into survival mode and gradually begin to abort our plans to work toward our goals. At this point so much of our time, attention, and energy is used on dealing with the things that are causing the frustration that we forget about our goals because we are simply on survival mode. And when this happens most of us have very little time or energy left to dedicate to reaching our goals or simply finishing what we started; we actually become inconsistent.

Since all of us only have only a limited amount of time and energy reserve, we should be mindful of what we dedicate our time and energy toward. So, in the midst of frustration, we still have to continue to move in the direction of reaching our goals in spite of the level of opposition. In order to maintain our focus and passion, we must learn to cope with all types of challenges to prevent frustration from changing our overall perspective on life. Instead of becoming frustrated when challenges come, we should learn to embrace them as a necessary part of the process of living a more balanced and fulfilling life.

### Peace Is Necessary

Where are you going, when should you go, and who should accompany you on the journey? These are some of the questions that we need answers to because much pain and great loss of sleep have occurred as a result of not having the right answers. We spend countless hours vacillating back and forth and wrestling with decisions that have frustrated us, stagnated our progress and even caused us to become procrastinators. Therefore, we are robbed of our peace and our ability to be objective thinkers who possess the gift of good decision making.

Let us think about this just for a moment to see how important peace and good objective decision making can be in our lives. According to Webster's Dictionary, peace is *"freedom from disquieting feelings and thoughts."* Hence, without peace, our minds are too cluttered and too busy to make objective decisions.

In today's fast-paced world, experiencing success and doing things that make us feel important are the order of the day. We actually believe that we are making progress when we fill our calendars up with meetings, when our emails are full, and when our cell phones are constantly ringing. We become so busy that we are only a fraction of the person we were created to be because we have no peace.

Whenever you don't have peace, you spend precious time wrestling in your mind and you can't make rational decisions. So it makes sense that peace is necessary to live a fulfilled, purposeful life. If you want to stop going around the same mountain, if you want to stop waking up every morning regretful about the night before, and if you want to stop ending up in the same old dead end work and social relationships, try something different this week. Take a few minutes prior to starting each day to write down your pending decisions and requests. Then tell God — specifically — everything you have written down.

I am not telling you that a miracle will take place nor am I telling you that this is a cure-all, but I am saying that this is the beginning of getting your peace back. The Bible says, *"Do not be anxious about anything, but in every situation, by prayer and petition, with thanksgiving, present your requests to God. And the peace of God, which transcends all understanding, will guard your hearts and your minds in Christ Jesus."* (Philippians 4:6-7 NIV)

## CHALLENGE

Spend some time thinking about some of your pending decisions and how they will impact the remainder of your life. You will discover that the quality of all your decisions are not found in books, friends, or television talk shows, but it is found in peace. Peace may not be a magical cure for all that you are going through, but it is necessary for making good, objective decisions.

CHAPTER 9

# Who Are You?

*"What is man, that thou art mindful of him and the son of man, that thou visitest him?"*

*Psalm 8:4 KJV*

There is one question that haunts most of us: Who am I? I am not talking about what neighborhood you live in, what kind of car you drive, what title is in front of your name, or how many degrees you may have. I am not talking about what church you attend or who your pastor is or what your social status is. I am simply talking about the person that few people get the opportunity to meet. I am talking about the man or woman in the mirror. As a matter of fact, you should really do a formal introduction to yourself, because for some of us this will be the very first time we meet. Most of us don't believe it, but we are exactly who we think we are.

As we move forward in our lives, we sometimes come to a place of confrontation. Most of us think that our biggest battles and confrontations take place on the job, with our spouse, or with jealous neighbors. Therefore, we spend endless hours coming up with the right strategy to overcome the obstacles that have been placed in our paths, and one battle at a time, we muster up enough strength to conquer and overcome these obstacles. And after overcoming these obstacles, we feel good about our victories. We have parties to celebrate our game plan coming together, only to find out that it's like chasing the wind. Just simply feeling good about our accomplishments is short-lived, and we start each new day strategizing about the battles ahead of us. This is an endless cycle that we repeat daily without dealing with the man or woman in the mirror. The biggest confrontation we will ever have is with the man or woman in the mirror. The one who has low self-esteem but dresses it up in expensive clothes; the one with the fear of rejection who is afraid to commit to anything or anyone; the one who thinks they don't measure up so they overachieve; or the one trying to live up to other people's expectations. These are the things that do more damage to us than any outside force could ever do. They shape our thinking in a way that impacts our destiny regardless of the image that we have created for ourselves.

Who are you? You are more than a conqueror, and you can do all things through Christ Jesus, who strengthens you. Just don't allow for situations and people to shape your thinking, but know that the key to success is being the person that God has destined you to be, which starts with a thought. The Bible says, *"For as he thinketh in his heart, so is he."* Proverbs 23:7 KJV

So who are you? You are exactly who you think you are; therefore you must begin to see yourself differently because other people will only see you as you see yourself. So instead of trying to fit into a role that was created for someone else, it's now time for you to step into your own. The real you has not come to the surface because you have only been acting or fulfilling a role that was created for you by someone else.

It amazes me how most people are living out other people's dreams for them instead of living their own dreams. I am reminded of the numerous times that I encountered situations where there was a breakdown in the parent-child relationship. The family came to me for counseling or advice on how to get the child back on the right track. And initially in my meeting with the family it looked as if the child had made an abrupt change from being a nice child to becoming a rebellious child, no longer interested in playing football, and failing in school. But after listening to the issues it became apparent that the child was not rebelling against their parents — they were rebelling against the dreams or plans that the parents had made for them.

So many of us are struggling because we are still trying to live out the plans that someone else drew up for our lives. As well-meaning as it may appear, you will never come to the conclusion of who you are by making choices and decisions that lines up with other people's dreams. You are unique, and there is no one else in the world like you. Sure, you may encounter people who look like you, act like you or who have similar character traits, but at the end of the day there is only one you. And I think that it's time for you to be formally introduced to you. Once you discover who you are, you will realize that no one on this earth can beat you at being you. At this point, you will never again have to ask the question "Who am I?"

There are two things in life that differentiate us from everyone else in the world and they are vision and destiny. Just like each person has a unique fingerprint, everyone has a unique vision and destiny. Your vision and your destiny are what set you apart from everyone else. That is why you can't walk in anyone else shoes or live out their dreams.

A vision is an act or power of anticipating that which will or may be; an insight of a future event. Most major inventions and discoveries were at one time simply ideas that rested in the hearts of men. They were isolated thoughts and matters of the heart that kept an individual from sleeping at night and made them uncomfortable. There was a constant feeling of being unfulfilled because they knew there was something they was supposed to be doing that would make life better for themselves and others. It was not necessarily money or success, as we have come to know, but instead a revolutionary idea that would only happen through connecting to others and the necessary resources. In the religious and business worlds we have made this idea a buzzword in hopes of motivating everyone to get on the same page: "vision." But vision it is more than a buzzword.

In this era most of us have minimized our own personal dreams because we have been lead to think that only CEOs and great leaders can have visions. We have reduced that tugging in our hearts to job-related or relationship stress, but it is more than stress. It is a personal vision inside of us that we must get out in the open because it is designed to connect us to others and change lives. Once we get over our fear of being ridiculed for having lofty dreams and begin to discuss our personal visions with others we will notice that it connects us to what others have been thinking about as well. And through this connection we will have more than enough resources to see our personal vision come to pass and change the lives of others in the process. We cannot let fear and procrastination keep us from acting upon our visions, because vision connects lives.

An architect is a good example of vision forming connections. When he connects with a person that wants to build something, he listens to their ideas and uses his skills to create a model of how the finished product will look. One person's ideas can become a reality through vision because it is his vision that connects him with other skills, resources, and relationships.

The Bible says in Proverbs 29:18 KJV, *"Where there is no vision, the people perish: but he that keepeth the law, happy is he."*

A vision is what gives meaning and purpose to your life; it motivates you and gives you something to strive for and in return it brings out the best in you. That's why Proverbs 29:18 says "without a vision the people perish" because without a dream or a vision we have nothing to look or work toward.

Destiny is not a person or a place but rather a hidden power believed to control what will happen in the future; it's fate. The path that the majority of us look for when embarking on the road to destiny is the one of least resistance. We have been led to think that we are on track for greatness when everything about our lives lines up in this orderly fashion that goes from success to success. As we peer through the window of history, we will notice that greatness and destiny rest right in the middle of the things that most of us are afraid to tackle. Instead of seeing the benefits of these challenges, most of us procrastinate or get too comfortable walking down the road of least resistance. We have learned how to sidestep life's defining challenges so well that we are now hiding from destiny.

Many of us have forfeited our right to greatness because we have settled for the comfort zone. We have placed so much emphasis on our material possessions, lifestyles, and reputations that we quake with fear when any of these are threatened by change. So as we go to great lengths to protect our material possessions, lifestyle, and reputations, we are actually hiding from our destiny.

The Bible says, *"This is what the Lord says – your Redeemer, the Holy One of Israel: 'I am the Lord your God, who teaches you what is best for you, who directs you in the way you should go. If only you had paid attention to my commands, your peace would have been like a river, your righteousness like the waves of the sea."* Isaiah 48:17-18 NIV.

Destiny is not a place, but it is adhering to a process that brings us face-to-face with our true purpose. Finally, we should also understand that in the midst of our vision and while moving towards our destiny we will come to the conclusion: "I know who I am."

## Just A Little Difference Can Lead to Destiny

I recently read an article on how to train an aging brain. It prompted me to think about how we make all types of New Year's resolutions in hopes of arriving at a point of positive change. Most of us are very sincere about changing our lives simply because we either don't like the results that we have gotten from our past actions or we know there is more inside of us that we have not tapped into yet. Over the past several years, scientists have looked deeper into how our brains age and confirmed that they continue to develop through and beyond middle age. The secret to change is not just making yearly resolutions, but we must come to a place of challenging some of our own assumptions, patterns, associations and long-held viewpoints we have worked so hard to accumulate while we were young. With our brain already full of well-connected pathways, as adult learners we should "jiggle our brains a bit" by embracing thoughts that are contrary to our own thoughts.

Most of us have become so comfortable with our friends, jobs, church, and level of education that we have become complacent. We never step outside of our comfort zone. Therefore, we stop growing, but more importantly, we are not challenged to think beyond what we already know. This is the type of thinking pattern that leads to repeating past mistakes, aborting New Year's resolutions or not doing things that will lead to a more productive lifestyle.

To grow mentally, we must initiate a continued brain development and a richer form of learning that may require us to "bump up against people and ideas" that are different than ours. We must learn to move beyond our present thinking patterns and challenge our perception of the world. If we always hang around only those we agree with and only read things that agree with what we already know, we're not going to wrestle with our old established brain connections. Such stretching is exactly what scientists say best keeps a brain in tune: get out of the comfort zone to push and nourish your brain. Do anything from learning a foreign language to taking a different route to work and you will be amazed that just a little change can lead you to your destiny.

The Bible says, *"Blessed is the man who finds wisdom, the man who gains understanding, for she is more profitable than silver and yields better returns than gold. She is more precious than rubies; nothing you desire can compare with her. Long life is in her right hand; in her left hand are riches and honor."* Proverbs 3:13- 16 (New International Version)

## CHALLENGE

This week, spend some time reevaluating your assumptions, patterns, associations, and long-held viewpoints. If you notice that week after week you only talk to people that agree with you and that you never move beyond your comfort zone to meet different people or do different things, you probably are not growing mentally. But if you do something different, you may just notice that a little difference may lead you to your destiny.

CHAPTER 10

# Understanding Your Purpose

*"Therefore, I urge you, brothers and sisters, in view of God's mercy, to offer your bodies as a living sacrifice, holy and pleasing to God this is your true and proper worship. Do not conform to the pattern of this world, but be transformed by the renewing of your mind. Then you will be able to test and approve what God's will is—his good, pleasing and perfect will."*

*Romans 12:1-2 NIV*

In order for any of us to achieve our life goals or for life to have any meaning, we must find our true God-given purpose. For so long, most of us have confused our true purpose with having some measure of success or obtaining material possessions, only to find out that neither achievements nor possessions can substitute for finding our true purpose in life.

Developing an understanding of the value of your true purpose is one of the key ingredients to living a life in which everything begins to make sense. The value of who you are, where you came from, where you are going, where you are at this point in your life, where you live, who your friends are, who you choose as a mate, and what you do for a living are all interconnected to your true purpose of life. It is through this higher level of consciousness that you begin to view and filter what you see, hear, and do on a daily basis in a more intentional manner.

The benefits of being more intentional will lead you to understand the value of synergy. In one of my favorite movies, The Godfather III, Al Pacino says, "Our ships must all sail in the same direction." That is, if he is going to get anything done, he must learn to allocate all of his available resources, relationships, and time in a cohesive manner flowing in the same direction or he must harness all of his resources to work toward the same goal. In simple terms, he needed synergy to get all of his energy moving in the same direction. Synergy is the interaction of elements that when combined produce a total effect that is greater than the sum of the individual elements or contributions working alone or in isolation. This approach is also known as systems thinking. Systems thinking is a language for describing and understanding the forces and interrelationships that shape the behavior of any type of systems. This discipline helps us view and filter what we see, and it empowers us to change how each system works in our life. During this process we can develop an approach that works more effectively, more efficiently, and more in tune with the natural processes or flow of any of our directed actions. Therefore, in order to understand and walk in our true-life purposes, we must understand the value of purpose, intention, synergy, and system thinking. So as you can see, living a life of purpose is much more than making a few positive confessions each day. It actually requires us to change or shift our entire mindset or change our way of thinking.

The Bible says, *"Therefore, I urge you, brothers and sisters, in view of God's mercy, to offer your bodies as a living sacrifice, holy and pleasing to God—this is your true and proper worship. Do not conform to the pattern of this world, but be transformed by the renewing of your mind. Then you will be able to test and approve what God's will is—his good, pleasing, and perfect will."* (Romans 12:1-2 NIV)

Most of us want to change how we live our lives, or we want good results from our efforts, but the majority of us are not willing to put in the necessary work to change or to live a life of true purpose. Therefore, we establish feel-good routines and simply get up every morning and stumble through our day hoping that we will luck out or happen up on a good opportunity that will make our life a little easier along the way. Ernest Holmes wrote in his book Science of Mind, "We live, then, as limited, crippled versions of who and what we were created to be because we don't understand our purpose for life."

Acquiring an objective understanding of the purpose of life

can be a daunting task that requires much thought, reflection, and energy, and can leave you starring into space without a clue of what is beyond the clouds. It's actually somewhat more challenging for those who refuse to look beyond our daily actions of getting up and going to work. Therefore, we must at some point begin to consider the fact that we are here for a reason and that there must be more to life than just being born and eventually dying.

When we think more objectively or spend some time pondering the purpose of life, we normally end up with more questions than answers. Therefore, instead of being able to come up with a definitive answer about the purpose of life, most of us find it so confusing and complex that we simply just give up. We give up on trying to find the right answer and become content simply existing instead of living—and there is a big difference between living and existing.

Existing is an objective reality and simply living under adverse conditions. Living or life is the condition that distinguishes animals and plants from inorganic matter, including the capacity for growth, reproduction, functional activity, and continual change preceding death.

As we can see, there is a striking difference between existing and living, as one is passive and the other active. Existing is related to being passive or allowing things to happen without responding actively with resistance. No work or actions are required to simply exist; all we have to do is have the basic things that are associated with life (food, water, air etc.). Simply existing has to be a boring and frustrating way to live. We have the ability to have and do more, but our passion to grow is lying dormant inside us. Yes, all of us are without excuse because we have the capacity to do and have more, which will become a reality as we tap into our true purpose for life. Therefore, simply existing is not a pre-existing condition based on race, educational status, or what side of the track we were born on—it is a choice. It is through the process of contemplation, critical thinking, and choices that we can move beyond simply existing to living a true life of purpose.

The Bibles says, *"This day I call the heavens and earth as witnesses against you that I have set before you life and death, blessings and curses. Now choose life, so that you and your children may live"* (Deuteronomy 30:19 NIV).

Whatever we do in life, mostly everything boils down to a matter of choice. We miss out on most of our opportunities to move closer to our goals and destiny because we either procrastinate or give up altogether when there is some level of opposition.

Living, on the other hand, is an active process that is connected to actions, discovery, mistakes, and the constant search to find the path that leads to our true purpose in life. Living is associated with being assertive, which means being self-confident, strong willed, and even sometimes domineering or pushy. Therefore, in order for us to find our true life purpose, we must be willing to move beyond any limitations, whether they are self-imposed or placed on us by others.

The purpose of life has to be viewed in two different aspects:

general and specific. A general purpose in life is an action or character trait that all men and women should display regardless of their sex, race, education, or socioeconomic level. Two of the general purposes of life are to treat all men with dignity and respect and to conduct oneself for the greater good of all men.

On the other hand, there are specific purposes of life that are different for each and every individual. A specific purpose is an assignment that has a definite or special application. Therefore, each person has a specific assignment that is unique in nature, and it usually lines up with their skillsets and true passions.

In the beginning of life as we know it, God communicated to man the purpose of life; however, our purpose does not become crystal clear to us all at once. So, in order for us to truly understand our purpose for being here on Earth and what we are to do while we are here, we must look to the only true source of truth: the Bible. The true purpose of life is to accept the fact that our existence started with God, recognize that He has a plan for our lives, and put forth our best effort daily to use the skills, resources, and relationships God has blessed us with.

One of the keys to living a life of purpose is to maintain a high level of God consciousness, which consists of the following:

1. Maintaining a relationship with God.
2. Practicing good stewardship and being a good manager of all that God has created that is within your reach.

In the beginning, the true purpose of life was brought into question, and man's relationship with God drastically changed.

Since that time man has been in pursuit of gaining back what was given to him in the beginning when God created man. Therefore, in order to clearly understand our true purpose, we must establish and maintain a relationship with God so that He can lead and guide us to all truth. We should always remember that a life without purpose is not living but simply existing.

## Outliers

We are living in a time when people spend most of their energy trying to fit into the mainstream of life. We like to dress like everyone else because it makes us appear to be keeping up with the style; we like to drive cars that have the approval of the masses; and we like to go to the places where we feel like we are part of the up-and-coming crowd. We rarely venture out into the deep because it makes us look different than most of our friends. In other words, we settle on being average in every way. It is this type of thinking that has made the study of statistics almost an exact science. After all, over time most people will repeat the same things. Therefore, statisticians can normally place the majority of the results of their human samplings into one box. But in the study of statistics there is also something that is known as an outlier (something that occurs outside the normal box), which is an observation that is numerically distant from the rest of the data.

In life there are men and women who do not fit into the mold of being average. They do things out of the ordinary. These people are called outliers because they think, act, and approach life differently than the average person. They are different in every way because their actions don't line up with normal statistical data. Hence, they are game changers. Outliers don't live their lives within the safe haven of mediocrity so they take risks, defy odds and do things that most people believe are impossible. Outliers are not giants but most people look at outliers like they are special or uniquely blessed. That is so far from the truth because we all can be outliers if we stop trying so hard to be average. The sad thing about being average is that average people are people who have the potential to be an outlier but they have settled for the lesser. The Bible says, *"Now unto Him that is able to do exceeding abundantly above all that we ask or think, according to the power that worketh in us, unto Him be glory in the church by Christ Jesus throughout all ages, world without end, Amen."* (Ephesians 3:20-21 KJV)

## CHALLENGE

Stop trying so hard to fit into the group, especially when it forces you to be just average. There is more inside of you waiting to come to the surface. However, it will only happen when you do something outside the box. Try becoming an outlier.

CHAPTER 11

# The Harvest

*"Now all has been heard; here is the conclusion of the matter: Fear God and keep his commandments, for this is the duty of all mankind. For God will bring every deed into judgment, including every hidden thing, whether it is good or evil."*

Ecclesiastes 12:13-14 NIV

At the conclusion of everything in life, we will simply find the sum total of every action, word, and thought. In other words, as we plant seeds of actions, words, and thoughts, there will always be some evidence of how we have lived our lives. Being unwilling to accept responsibility or accountability for our actions, words, and thoughts does not mean that they will somehow not come into judgment at some point. I think Sir Isaac Newton said it best when he said, "For every action, there is an equal and opposite reaction." Although he was talking about contact interactions, the principle is still the same.

It is vitally important for us to understand that there are benefits or consequences for everything we do in life, and there are no exceptions to this rule. Sure, there are times when grace or unmerited favor enters into the picture and we don't get exactly what we deserve; however, that does not change or alter the overall principle. The principle is that we reap what we sow, and it is the same in every aspect of our lives. I think when we look at it from a farmer's perspective, it is easily understood. Most farmers who I have met clearly understand the sowing and reaping principle. If they planted tomato seeds during planting season, they were not looking for a harvest of corn. It is a clear picture of the sowing and reaping principle. Most of us don't look at our lives in this way. We feel as if we have a right to plant tomato seeds and look for corn in return, which causes us to act in a very irresponsible manner. This type of thinking has caused most of us to make some very poor decisions that are still affecting our lives today. Some of these decisions have affected our lives slightly, and there is room to recuperate or bounce back after being left with just a small scar as a reminder. On the other hand, there are some decisions that have affected our lives in a more profound way, and it takes longer to bounce back from these. Instead of having just a small scar, we may be left with a noticeable limp as a result of this poor decision. Finally, there are some decisions that we make that are so drastic that it may take a lifetime to recover—and in some instances, there is no recovery. Looking at our lives from this perspective will make us more responsible for how we live on a daily basis.

As we increase our level of awareness of how our lives are affected on a daily basis by our actions, words, and thoughts, we should come to a place of being more intentional in the types of choices we make. We have been blessed with the intellectual capital to be able to reason, analyze, and investigate every situation and judge what type of return we will get from each and every decision. Even though we underestimate and underutilize our intellectual capital, we have the necessary tools to contemplate and use critical thinking to make better choices. Since we don't use our intellectual capital or maximize its use, most of us spend a great deal of our lives, time, and energy recovering from mistakes. Because we spend so much time in recovery mode, we have little time or energy left to work toward fulfilling our God-given destiny. As I mentioned earlier, everybody likes a good comeback story, and there is something about a comeback story that touches all of us, however, I think most comeback stories leave out a vital part. While most of the time we celebrate the comeback, we miss the potential of where a person could have been if not for the bump in the road. We also underestimate the toll or the long-term impact of having gone through some of the things that came as a result of losing our focus, hanging with the wrong crowd, or investing our time and energy into the wrong things. I once heard a man say that there is no such thing as overnight success. He further clarified, saying, "Success is not a one time event; it is a lifetime process." In other words, it appears easy to others, but it is harder than it seems.

As I mentioned in an earlier chapter, most of us are not patient, therefore, we have arrived at a place of thinking that is called the "microwave mindset," believing that things could change at the drop of a hat. This microwave mindset has led most of us to think that success will come overnight or that we can recover overnight from bad decision-making. It is this type of thinking that has a great deal of people looking to God to rescue them from their situation or for a miracle, and if He does not give them a miracle something is wrong. Yes, there is something wrong, but nothing is wrong with God. Rather, something is wrong with how we think. Since God is so loving, He would never impose His will on anyone to do things they don't want to do. Instead, He has given us free will, or the right of choice. And since we have the right of choice we also have to accept the responsibility that comes with that type of freedom. This is a good indication that although we will encounter some circumstances and challenges that we did not ask for, at the end of the day, our life is shaped more by our actions, words, thoughts, and decisions than we care to admit. As the Word reminds us, *"This day I call the heavens and earth as witnesses against you that I have set before you life and death, blessings and curses. Now choose life, so that you and your children may live"* (Deuteronomy 30:19 NIV).

The right of choice is so powerful that it shapes the course of our lives on a daily basis and minimizes the idea that one experience or one incident is responsible for our current place in life. One of my favorite scriptures in the Bible truly opened up my eyes to the role of transformation and led me to the place of making small incremental changes in my life on a daily basis: *"Do not conform to the pattern of this world, but be transformed by the renewing of your mind. Then you will be able to test and approve what God's will is—his good, pleasing and perfect will"* (Romans 12:2 NIV).

This scripture helped me understand the importance of daily growth instead of trying to change overnight. Trying to change everything at one time can be an overwhelming task. One day someone asked me, "How do you eat an elephant?" I said it is impossible to eat an elephant because of its enormous size. The person replied to me with a very simple but yet profound statement: "You can eat an elephant by simply taking one bite at a time."

As indicated in Romans 12:2, most of our lives are lived by following the patterns that have been set by others—and usually when we follow this pattern, we get the same type of results. If we want something different than the status quo for our lives then we have to start the process of changing our actions, words, thoughts, and decisions.

There are some things in life that will keep you frustrated, that will render you unable to give your undivided attention to the things that will shape the outcome of your life. These things I would like to say are disturbers of your harmony, and they interfere with your ability to make rational decisions. These disturbers will cause you to make quick and thoughtless decisions because you are not operating at your best from a neurological or mental perspective. It is proven by neurologists that when our brains are invaded by negative thoughts, stress, and fear, a chemical is released into the brain that makes it almost impossible to be rational in that moment. However, if our brains are invaded by positive thoughts, happiness, and peace, then the brain releases a different chemical that gives us access to the gateway of our higher cognitive functioning.

To change how you think and ultimately how you act, it is important for you to remove yourself from stressful and negative environments and relationships. As I stated earlier, it is the small, incremental changes that eventually lead to wholesome changes in our lives. Therefore, just simply removing yourself from stressful environments and stressful relationships is a major change that can lead to you being able to contemplate, use your critical thinking skills, and ultimately make better choices. Sure, it is easy to blame someone else for your place in life, but the conclusion of the matter is that every one of your deeds will be called into judgment and will determine your outcome in life.

## What Type of Seeds Are You Planting?

When we think in terms of sowing seeds, most of us automatically think about money. Money should be associated with sowing, but it is not the only thing that we should be thinking about when using this principle. We miss out on so much of our life's harvest because we have failed to use the seed-sowing principle in every area of our lives. We actually live life being only a limited crippled version of who we were created to be because we fail to reap an abundant harvest that comes from sowing into the lives of others.

Most of us never reach our full potential, and we play a vital part in others not reaching their full potential either because we fail to make valuable deposits into them. We have become such much a selfish generation of people who spend so much time focusing on ourselves we cannot see the potential in others. This type of blindness has contributed to the overall under functioning in our families, communities, and local churches. We all suffer as result of not sowing seeds into the lives of others and we also deny ourselves from receiving an abundant harvest of a fulfilled life.

It's time for us to stop being so critical of others who may not be living up to their full potential and let's start making the type of deposits that could change their lives. Duplicate yourself by mentoring someone, by exposing them to a different life, by encouraging them to follow their dreams, by encouraging them to go back to school, or just by being a constant positive presence in their lives. The Bible says, *"Remember this; the person who sows sparingly will also reap sparingly, and the person who sows generously will also reap generously. Each person should do as he has decided in his heart – not out of regret or out of necessity, for God loves a cheerful giver. And God is able to make every grace overflow to you, so that in every way, always having everything you need, you may excel in every good work"* (II Corinthians 9:6-8 HCSB Version).

## CHALLENGE

Spend some time thinking about someone in your immediate circle who needs some help. Ask yourself what type of seeds you are sowing to help that person or others.

CHAPTER 12

# It's All a Matter of Choice

*"Do not be deceived: God is not mocked, for whatever one sows, that will he also reap."*

*Galatians 6:7*

There will come a time in all of our lives when we will have to come face to face with some of our past decisions. We will either reap the good benefits of those choices or we will have to deal with the consequences of our poor choices. Either way, at the end of the day, we will realize that it's all a matter of choice.

Some of us have procrastinated or delayed the process of making certain decisions, and because we failed to act or make a decision, we ended up getting the same results as we did when we made a poor choice. Either way, everything we will ever deal with in life boils down to one simple thing: It's all a matter of choice.

One of the hardest things to face is that you have almost everything to do with the place you are in life. Yes, it was you, not your haters or the devil, but your choices have shaped your life into what it is right now. This is a very difficult thing to grasp because we have talked ourselves into believing that outside forces or environmental influences we encounter have shaped our lives. However, we should know that no outside influence or power has more control over our thoughts than we do. Sure, they may influence us or affect us in some way, but in spite of that, we have the final say over what we do and our decisions.

So instead of looking for somewhere to place the blame for our current place in life, we should become more proactive and start the process of initiating a change in the way we make key life decisions. We must come up with a consistent way of implementing new disciplines that will not overwhelm our efforts to change our lives so that we can make better decisions. For most of us, we have come to the conclusion that change is necessary, but how to implement this change is a different story altogether. It is important to know that change is not a miraculous set of events that take place overnight, but it is a process. It is proven that it is easier to make incremental changes than wholesale changes because when we try to overcome all of our weaknesses at once, it's like trying to eat an elephant with just one bite. Just like trying to eat an elephant in one bite is impossible, likewise, it is also impossible to change everything about ourselves all at once. On the other hand, if we begin the process of learning to apply new disciplines into our life on a daily basis, it can lead to a tremendous amount of change.

The amazing thing about our choices is that the majority of people have been led to think that the influence or actions of others has more of a profound impact on their lives than their own personal choices. Therefore, we spend a great deal of time and energy trying to change others and very little time trying to change how we go about making important life decisions. We should also be mindful that there is no miracle cure to correct our past bad decisions and that the decisions that we will make on today will be more responsible for shaping our future than anything else.

What does it mean to have the right of choice? A choice is the power, right, or liberty to choose or having options. This is a clear indication that being able to choose is a power that is given to us to shape the outcome of our lives, however, most of us neglect to exercise this power. Therefore, when we fail to make good choices we forfeit the opportunity or give up the right to control our own destiny. And when this happens we are left at the mercy of others and we become codependent upon them to do for us what we have been empowered to do ourselves. Besides becoming codependent upon others to help shape our destiny we also start to place unrealistic expectations upon others to make us happy, bail us out of situations or give us advice on how we should make key life decisions. However, I have learned that the more codependent we are upon others, the more we tend to blame others for our choices or when things in our lives veer off course. This type of thinking shifts the burden of responsibility off of the individual whose life is actually being affected. Now they have a justification for failure or an excuse for not living up to their full life potential. Often times when we engage others in conversation who may be experiencing some life challenges, we can hear if they are accepting responsibility for their own life or if they are shifting the blame to others.

Most of us carry around a list of excuses in our pockets that makes us feel better about ourselves. This list of excuses is like a hall pass that was given to a child when they were in grade school. Therefore, when one of the school administrators saw them in the hallway they simply showed the administrator the hall pass and he gave them a pass for being out of place. Yes, some of us simply just reach in our pockets and pull out our hall pass when our life is out of place or when we are not living up to our potential. We wave this pass like a badge of honor and become comfortable under-functioning. We should stop blaming people, places and things for where we are in life because an excuse is simply just a legal right or justification to fail. We don't have to live our life in constant fear of failure or constantly blaming others. It's time to take control of your own life, starting with taking ownership of your decisions.

Although we have the power of choice most people don't execute or act upon this awesome power, therefore, this awesome power lays buried underneath the surface like a volcano that is ready to erupt at any given moment. Yes, you are adequate and you have the power to overcome anything but it does not start from blaming; it all starts with acceptance. Accepting the fact that I am where I am in my life because of the choices I have made, and if I want my circumstances to change, I must be willing to change how I go about making key life decisions. It's all a matter of choice.

Most of the decisions that we make are emotional decisions. Instead of doing our due diligence, most of us make key life decisions based on how we feel. Although our feelings change constantly, we place our future and the future of those who are an important part of our lives in the hands of our emotions. Very little thought goes into our decisions because most of us are held prisoners of the moment. However, your future is too important to make decision simply based on how you may feel. Far too often, we find ourselves in dilemmas that alter the course of our lives because we did not do our due diligence. Instead, we just forge ahead and make a decision because it felt good, never taking into consideration the long-term impact of that one decision. Therefore, we are constantly fighting against ourselves when we make emotional decisions, using valuable time and resources going around the same mountain. For most of us, instead of moving forward in our lives, we spend the majority of our time going around in circles. We end back up in the same place that we started from, making no progress at all.

Most of us are creatures of habit. We repeat the same poor decision-making process day in and day out, yet we expect different results. Even though the writing is on the wall and we know what the results will be in a situation, we still forge ahead, making one poor life-altering choice after another. As I stated earlier, as a result of this, we find ourselves in a place that looks all too familiar, and although, we are frustrated and tired of the results, we continue to go back to that familiar place of making bad decisions.

Instead of continuing this process of making poor decisions that open the door to stress, depression, and anxiety, we can begin the process of implementing change into our lives so that we can make better choices and decisions that will lead to living a more balanced and fulfilled life. Instead of being negatively influenced by others or being held captive in the moment that results in poor decisions, we can work toward becoming more thoughtful with each and every decision.

**Contemplation, critical thinking** and **choices** are a good way to start making each and every decision we are faced with daily. This method will work in any type of decision – whether the decision is small or large, financial or even a relationship decision. *Contemplation means to look thoughtfully at something for a long time; think profoundly and at length; or even to meditate.* The answer to your situation is not in how fast you make a decision. We should allow for life to slow down long enough to take the necessary time to explore all facets of each pending decision. It would not hurt to pull away from our daily routine long enough to calm the raging sea of problems that are swirling around in order to meditate. Meditation is simply to engage in mental exercise for the purpose of reaching a heightened level of spiritual, emotional or intellectual awareness. In meditation, you can focus your thoughts on your situation and move beyond your surface thoughts to gain greater insight on the multiple options that you have at your disposal.

Critical thinking is vitally necessary to make any type of decision. Critical thinking is totally opposite of emotional thinking and affords you to look beyond your feelings and engage in a higher form of thinking. *Critical thinking is also a mode of thinking — about any subject, content, or problem — in which the thinker improves the quality of his or her thinking by intentionally analyzing, assessing, and reframing his or her thoughts about a situation.* Because our decisions are so influenced by our previous decisions and their outcomes, we have to take the time reframe our thoughts so that we can see things differently. Critical thinking is required in every decision because every decision you make is critical to living a balanced and more fulfilled life.

Our choices are the seeds that we plant in our gardens, and the types of seeds that we plant have everything to do with the type of harvest that we will get out of life. Having the right and ability to choose is a level of empowerment that supersedes any outside forces that try to influence our thoughts. *Choosing is the act of picking or deciding between two or more possibilities or the opportunity or power to make a decision.* Each person has the power to make better choices that will change his or her circumstances and afford the person an opportunity to live a more balanced and fulfilling life. Remember, that it's all a matter of choice.

## It's Okay to Spend Some Time Alone

The days of solitude and peace seem to be a thing of the past because we rarely find time to be alone. We have so much vying for our attention that we think that something is wrong with us if we are not doing something or being with someone. This type of thinking has caused many of us to do things and connect to people that were not in our best interest. We end up compromising who we are because we have not learned how to be alone.

Most of us have been equating the word "lonely" with a person that does not have a significant other or someone who is not showing up at every social event. However, that is far from the truth. Also, the word "alone" seems to have such a negative connotation attached to it that most people are looking for something to do or for someone to be with just to keep from being alone. As a result of being afraid to be alone we end up living a life that appears to be one big happy party, but the truth of the matter is we are really miserable.

It is time to stop compromising who you really are by doing things that you really don't want to do, going places that you really don't want to go, and being with people that you really don't want to be with. Yes, it's time to take a moment to be alone and reflect, reevaluate and meditate, listening to the inner man who is always speaking.

## CHALLENGE

Take some time to be alone so that you can be refreshed for the journey of life. Remember, if you are not alone, you may not be able to hear. Besides, you are never really alone because God is always with you. The Bible says, *"The Lord himself goes before you and will be with you; he will never leave you nor forsake you. Do not be Version afraid; do not be discouraged"* (Deuteronomy 31:8 NIV).

# Conclusion

The ability to move in concert with our God-given abilities starts with recognizing the fact that we have more power than we have been led to think. This has been an ongoing problem for people who are underachievers or for people dealing with the majority of life's problems.

Most of us have gone through life not being keenly aware of who we are and the power that we have resident inside. Therefore, since we don't know who we are, we are being destroyed from a lack of knowledge by making one poor choice after another. The power of choice is something that affords us the opportunity to move beyond any self-imposed limitations and allow for us to focus on our destiny. One of my favorite Scriptures does a good job of explaining the correlation between knowledge and power:

*"My people are destroyed for lack of knowledge. Because thou hast rejected knowledge, I will also reject thee, that thou*

shalt be no priest to Me. Seeing thou hast forgotten the law of thy God, I will also forget thy children" (Hosea 4:6 NIV).

Also, understanding and being able to properly exercise your power of choice also eliminates the pseudo power that others have exercised in your life by influencing your decisions. This places you in a position to accept responsibility for your own decisions but more importantly places you control of your own destiny.

I pray that this book has a profound impact on your life and that you will apply these principles to your daily life. Always remember that knowledge is not power unless you apply it enough to change your circumstance. Ultimately, applying knowledge will change your life through wiser choices.

www.ingramcontent.com/pod-product-compliance
Lightning Source LLC
Chambersburg PA
CBHW070625300426
44113CB00010B/1657